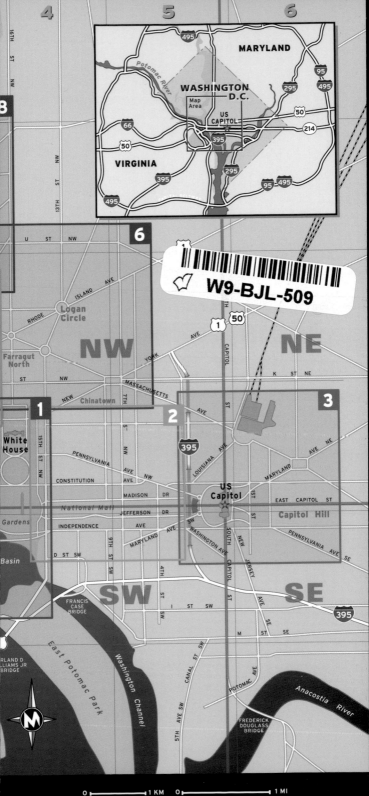

MOON METRO
WASHINGTON D.C.

CONTENTS

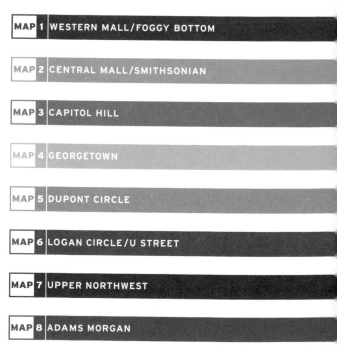

AVALON Ⓐ TRAVEL

HOW TO USE THIS BOOK

MAP SECTION

- We've divided Washington D.C. into eight distinct areas. Each area has been assigned a color, used on the map itself and in easy-to-spot map number indicators throughout the listings.

- The maps show the location of every listing in the book, using the icon that indicates what type of listing it is (sight, restaurant, etc.) and the listing's locator number.

- The coordinates (in color) indicate the specific grid that the listing is located in. The black number is the listing's locator number. The page number directs you to the listing's full description.

MAP 1 WESTERN MALL / FOGGY BOTTOM

LISTINGS SECTION

- The listings are organized into six sections:
  - ❶ SIGHTS
  - ❷ RESTAURANTS
  - ❸ NIGHTLIFE
  - ❹ SHOPS
  - ❺ ARTS AND LEISURE
  - ❻ HOTELS

- Within each section, the listings are organized by which map they are located in, then in alphabetical order.

MAP 1 WESTERN MALL/FOGGY BOTTOM

THE BOMBAY CLUB *BUSINESS • INDIAN $$*
The Bombay Club wins hearts and return business with its gently seasoned Indian cooking, contemporary and elegant environs, and affordable prices. Despite many competitors, the Bombay Club remains a downtown favorite for lunches, dinners, and Sunday brunches.

MAP 1 A5 ❶ 11   815 CONNECTICUT AVE. NW
202-659-3727

BREAD LINE *CAFÉ $*
Just steps from the White House, Bread Line, with its frantic pace and disorderly interior, plays host to Washington's premiere power breakfast. Spot your favorite spin doctors behind the pages of The Washington Post as you sip fresh orange juice and grab a quick croissant.

MAP 1 A5 ❶ 13   1751 PENNSYLVANIA AVE. NW

CAFÉ ASIA *HOT SPOTS • PAN-ASIAN $$*
A sleek, curved bar, well-priced sushi, and an array of carnivore- and vegetarian-friendly Asian plates make this downtown mainstay a favorite happy hour stopover. The decibels sometimes reach rock concert levels, but the young, carefree crowd doesn't seem to mind.

MAP 1 A5 ❶ 8   1720 I ST. NW
202-659-2696

EQUINOX *HOT SPOTS • AMERICAN $$$*
Chef and owner Todd Gray has created a unique restaurant with a front garden room that complements the dressier interior seating. Its proximity to the White House means big names lunch and dine here, enjoying inventive American cooking such as the spiced Virginia hanger steak with braised kale.

MAP 1 A5 ❶ 10   818 CONNECTICUT AVE. NW
202-331-8118

KINKEAD'S *BUSINESS • SEAFOOD $$$*
This wood-paneled power spot unveiled a fresh look in February 2004 with a new kitchen and swankier mood lighting. Choose between comforting favorites like lobster pie and zesty fish stew from the updated seafood menu, and the Ipswich clams, still an establishment favorite, are a must try.

MAP 1 A4 ❶ 6   2000 PENNSYLVANIA AVE. NW
202-296-7700

NECTAR *BUSINESS • NEW AMERICAN $$$*
Cozy and simple, Nectar is the rare restaurant that manages to combine neighborhood friendliness with urban elegance. A good bet for pre-Kennedy Center dining, the ever-changing menu offers progressive New American cuisine that is as dazzling as any theater performance. Try the luscious pheasant or crab with melon and avocado.

MAP 1 A2 ❶ 2   824 NEW HAMPSHIRE AVE. NW
202-298-8085

22 MOON METRO

← → TWO WAYS TO NAVIGATE

1. Scan the map to see what listings are in the area you want to explore. Use the directory to find out the name and page number for each listing.

2. Read the listings to find the specific place you want to visit. Use the map information at the bottom of each listing to find the listing's exact location.

MAP KEY

Major Sights	★
Metro Stop	Ⓜ
Shopping District	
Stairs	ⅢⅢⅢⅢ
Pedestrian Street	
Adjacent Map Boundaries	SEE MAP 1 ▷

SECTION ICONS

- ✪ SIGHTS
- ® RESTAURANTS
- Ⓝ NIGHTLIFE
- Ⓢ SHOPS
- Ⓐ ARTS AND LEISURE
- Ⓗ HOTELS

B1 17 Roof Terrace Restaurant & Bar, p. 23

ROOF TERRACE RESTAURANT & BAR
BUSINESS • NEW AMERICAN $$$

Inside the Kennedy Center, this glam restaurant affords its patrons a dazzling view of the Potomac River. The staid chandeliers have been replaced with shiny glass columns and the modern American menu has been kicked up a notch, with short ribs, duck breast, and tasty crab cakes.

MAP 1 B1Ⓡ17 KENNEDY CENTER, 2700 F ST. NW
202-416-8555

Use the **MAP NUMBER, COLOR GRID COORDINATES**, and **BLACK LOCATOR NUMBER** to find the exact location of every listing in the book.

INTRODUCTION TO
WASHINGTON D.C.

Washington D.C. is a city of low-rise buildings and skyscraper-size egos. It is a place where campaign managers get rock star treatment, every barroom TV in town is tuned to CNN, and even your cab driver is anxious to talk politics. It's a city without a state, with taxation (but without representation), and where all roads literally lead to Capitol Hill, the city center. In many ways, the place is a riddle. And if you're here in August, the joke will be on you: Washington was built on a swamp, so central air-conditioning will seem more important than a voter registration card.

The city is also the gateway to the South, with acres of public parkland and historic estates. John F. Kennedy once complained about the city's "Southern efficiency," but that was a while ago. The corporate culture here demands that things run like military clockwork. The Metro is spotless and punctual, and every rush hour many heavily traveled streets become one-way – to the relief of local commuters and to the confusion of frazzled out-of-towners. It's also not unusual to see checkpoints in front of important buildings. Security has been ramped up since September 11, 2001, and the rattle of military Humvees and the buzz of low-flying helicopters are now just background noise for unfazed residents.

Despite the trauma of 9/11, Washington has settled back into a routine. Government workers often clock out by 6 P.M., and downtown's streets tend to clear out. Power players duck into expense-account dining rooms, people young and old crowd the Mall to play volleyball or base-

D.C.'S HEART AND SOUL

Politics might drive Washington's mind, but its heart and soul belong to the African American tradition. More than 60 percent of the city's residents are black, and their heritage predates the District's founding in 1791. As a Southern city, Washington once held slave markets on what is now the National Mall. Decades later, Georgetown was a prominent stop on the Underground Railroad. In the 20th century, civil rights rallies electrified the city.

Today, this heritage is preserved in many sights, such as the African American Civil War Memorial that lists every black American who fought in that war, and the Lincoln Memorial, where Martin Luther King Junior's "I Have a Dream" speech is etched on the steps. The rich tradition also steers the city's cultural life. Washington swells with world-class jazz and blues clubs, shops selling traditional African clothing and furniture, and museums dedicated to African American history, music, and even fashion. The country's best Ethiopian and Eritrean food is served in Adams Morgan — just steps from the Duke Ellington Bridge, named after one of D.C.'s most famous sons.

ball, and others begin the trek back uptown. Many residents step out of the Metro at Dupont Circle or Adams Morgan, areas full of bars, shops, and ethnic restaurants of every persuasion. In these vibrant neighborhoods, with dignified townhouses on every corner and sidewalks teeming with businesspeople, briefcases in hand and cell phones glued to ear, it might seem that there is no limit to the wealth and power concentrated here.

On the other side of the Capitol, however, the neighborhoods of Northeast and Southeast Washington struggle in its shadow. Many people never venture to this side of the city, alarmed by constant reports of violent crime. Those who do will find some of Washington's most beautiful rowhouses, best Southern restaurants, and lush gardens standing next to crumbling buildings and vacant lots. Residents are fiercely loyal to their neighborhoods, and many families have been here for generations, regardless of who's in office.

But the bulk of the major sights are back in North- and Southwest, where D.C. seems like an orderly city of energetic transients. Year after year, bright-eyed idealists

arrive ready to change the world. Many do, and many end up moving on after leaving their mark. So the faces pouring through the streets change every few years, each wanting to influence legislation, pass this bill, seal that deal. Meanwhile, the Washington Monument, the White House, the Capitol – icons that have welcomed generations of young hopefuls – stand tall in all their grandeur, patiently waiting for the next world leader to arrive.

HISTORY

Washington D.C. began as – what else? – a political disagreement. After the Revolutionary War, Northerners favored New York City or Philadelphia as the center of power. But Southern politicians wanted a capital closer to them and offered up land and money to get their way. If the Northern states agreed to establish the capital farther south, it was decided, the federal government would assume the war debts of all the states. In the end, Congress approved the Compromise of 1790, and Charles-Pierre L'Enfant designed Washington D.C. in a then-innovative grid system. John Adams was the first president to live in the Executive Mansion, which was constantly under construction during his presidency – as was much of the city.

For years afterward Washington was a quiet town with a tiny population, but it began to look and feel like a modern city after the Civil War. The population swelled, monuments were built, and the stage was set for the city to become the backdrop for the tumultuous 20th cen-

INSIDE THE BELTWAY

The Beltway is a highway that encircles Washington, and life inside it radiates around politics and government. Most people here are somehow affiliated with one or the other, making D.C. a company town: buzzing by 9 A.M., ready for bed by 10 or 11 at night. Local gossips may not care about Paris Hilton, but the goings-on at the Capital Hilton's White House Correspondents Dinner, on the other hand, is a perennial hot topic. Neither is Washington an overly stylish place, and edgy fashion statements are rare. Political statements, however, never go out of style. So don't come to D.C. in your Prada armor. Instead, come with ideas.

tury. The National Mall was a prime protest scene during the Civil Rights struggle and the Vietnam War, and Martin Luther King's "I Have a Dream" speech became immortal at the Lincoln Memorial in 1963. Watergate was a historic moment of a different kind, and the chic hotel-office complex that helped ruin Richard Nixon in 1974 still stands. Today, D.C. is a booming metropolis surrounded by endless suburban sprawl, still rich with political squabbles and plenty of scandal.

DON'T SNACK AND RIDE

Most everyone gets around on the Metro, D.C.'s subway system, which is clean, efficient, and nearly always punctual. By and large, Metro stations are safe — except for snackers. Eating, drinking, smoking, and littering are prohibited, and Metro officials are always on alert for violations. Police have detained travelers caught eating inside stations or onboard the train. One rider was arrested for unwrapping a candy bar while on an escalator and refusing to discard it. The results of this vigilance are visible: The platforms and surrounding areas are spotless.

WASHINGTON MONUMENT

SMITHSONIAN

LINCOLN MEMORIAL

THE BEST OF
WASHINGTON D.C.

With all that D.C. has to offer, a day in the capital can mean breakfasting among White House staffers, viewing the newest memorial on the Mall, touching a moon rock, and enjoying dinner at a talk-of-the-town restaurant. Here is a day that samples classic D.C., full of those must-see landmarks that still take even native Washingtonians by pleasant surprise. Breathtaking sights like the Washington Monument and the Lincoln Memorial have long been necessary stops for any visitor. And an afternoon at one of the Smithsonian museums is worth about a year in college — and costs a lot less money, too.

1 Have a quintessential Washington breakfast at the **Old Ebbitt Grill (p. 26)** downtown, where the power players often meet before doing business.

2 Work off your meal with a stroll down Pennsylvania Avenue to the gates of the **White House (p. 6)** for some choice photo opportunities from the Ellipse.

3 From the White House, the National Mall is a quick and scenic walk. If it's open and there are still tickets, be sure to take a ride to the top of the **Washington Monument (p. 5)** for a panoramic view of the city.

4 Explore the western part of the Mall's many monuments and memorials – the new-in-2004 **National World War II Memorial (p. 2)** is a must. Afterward, grab a quick lunch from one of the many vendors scattered around the perimeter – they sell everything from pizza and hot dogs to egg rolls.

5 At the opposite end of the Mall is the **Smithsonian (p. 10).** Spend the afternoon exploring one or two of its several branches. The **National Air and Space Museum (p. 8)** is always a favorite, but if you can't stand the crowds, try the **National Museum of the American Indian (p. 71).**

6 Within walking distance of the Mall is a timeless Washington watering hole: **Sky Terrace (p. 44)** at the Hotel Washington. Sip drinks on the rooftop terrace April-October while watching the sun set over the city. During the colder months, step into the chic bar at **Butterfield 9 (p. 23)** instead.

7 After drinks, walk up to **Ceiba (p.24),** one of the hottest restaurants in town, for a Latin-tinged meal.

8 Take a cab back toward the National Mall area for a look at the monuments after dark. The **Lincoln Memorial (p. 2)** is luminescent at night, not to mention less crowded.

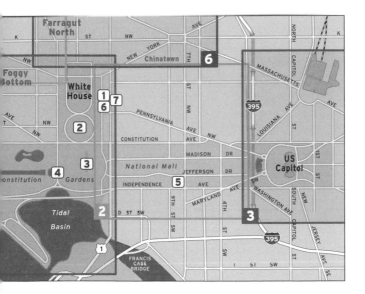

KRAMERBOOKS & AFTERWORDS   KUNA

MELLOW
WASHINGTON

With the lobbyists on K Street, the politicians on the Hill, and the hordes of tourists at the monuments and museums, Washington is, to a large degree, a high-powered destination. But this buttoned-up city is starting to loosen its tie upon occasion. Sleek boutique hotels, like Hotel Helix, and trendy restaurants, like those on U Street, have recently been popping up around town, and it is possible to spend a full day in the city without visiting a single monument. Of course, some institutions in Washington have never gone out of style, like the venerable jazz venue HR-57 and the late-night, heartburn-inducing Ben's Chili Bowl.

1 Book a room at **Hotel Helix (p. 94),** a swank retro property near Logan Circle.

2 Stroll toward Dupont Circle, and grab brunch on the patio of **Kramerbooks & Afterwords (p. 32),** a favorite hipster hangout. After eating, browse through the bookstore – the travel and cookbook sections are particularly notable.

3 Spend the morning shopping **Dupont Circle (p. 59),** with its chic boutiques and upmarket chains. In this area, you'll also find a bead shop and the city's funkiest record store.

4 Continue your retail therapy with a walk up **18th Street (p. 65)** to check out Adams Morgan's many eclectic shops, where the items on offer range from the latest fashions to antique doorknobs.

5 Washington has some of the best Ethiopian restaurants in the country, and many of them are in Adams

Morgan. Savor an authentic lunch at **Meskerem (p. 40)** on 18th Street.

6 The **National Zoo (p. 19)** is an easy walk or short cab ride from the restaurant. Spend a relaxing afternoon visiting with the pandas and baby tigers.

7 Catch the Metro at Woodley Park, and take it to U Street/Cardozo. Peek in the windows of the funky boutiques along U Street on the way to **Kuna (p. 35)** for a cozy Italian dinner.

8 After dinner, duck into **Café Saint Ex/Gate 54 (p. 48)** for drinks at the polished bar or in the chill downstairs lounge, before heading to jazz institution HR-57, where it's BYOB.

9 Named after a House resolution to make jazz a national treasure, **HR-57 (p. 80)** showcases amazing live music.

10 Before heading to bed, satisfy late-night hunger pangs with a hot dog or chili from **Ben's Chili Bowl (p. 35),** an eye-opener at any hour of the night.

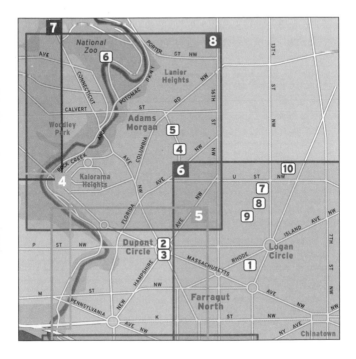

GEORGETOWN | INTERNATIONAL SPY MUSEUM

SCANDALOUS
WASHINGTON

Scandal and intrigue have enshrouded Washington since its early days as the capital city, when shocked locals whispered about Abigail Adams hanging her laundry in the unfinished East Room of the White House. Over the years, the topics of rumor and investigation have ranged from the everyday affairs of Senators to executive-level cover-ups to international espionage. The following offers a glimpse into the underworld of Washington, from Georgetown, home of many high-profile power players, to an evening at Ford's Theatre, where Lincoln spent his final night on the town.

1 Begin your day in **Georgetown (p. 57),** home to many of Washington's politicians and spies. Alger Hiss, the focus of a notorious espionage case in the late 1940s, is among the significant figures who have lived here. Spend the morning shopping along M Street, where upscale boutiques and historic rowhouses stand side by side.

2 Enjoy a civilized Italian lunch at **Café Milano (p. 29),** a beloved haunt for Washington's "cave dwellers," – a nickname for those who have been established in the city for generations. This is a favorite of local socialites, so try to listen for some hot gossip.

3 Take the Metro from Foggy Bottom to Gallery Place-Chinatown for an afternoon at D.C.'s homage to scandal and intrigue: the **International Spy Museum (p. 70).** History, gadgets, and video of former spies are displayed in the fascinating exhibits here. Stop by the museum store to make some of the secret-agent fantasy your own. Also on the premises is the museum's spy-themed lounge and restaurant, Zola. Have a drink — make sure no one's watching you.

4 Dine early at **La Colline (p. 28),** a reliable French restaurant on Capitol Hill. From the museum, take the Metro to Union Station or get a cab. Close to the Senate office buildings, this restaurant is where generations of staffers have rendezvoused — for business or otherwise.

5 Cap off the day with a show at **Ford's Theatre (p. 78),** where Abraham Lincoln was shot. (The 16th president's death did not actually take place in the theater, but in a house across the street.) John Wilkes Booth is known as the assassin by school children across the land, but was there a larger conspiracy at work?

6 After the play, hop a cab back to your hotel, which, if you're a true scandal enthusiast, is the infamous **Watergate (p. 90).**

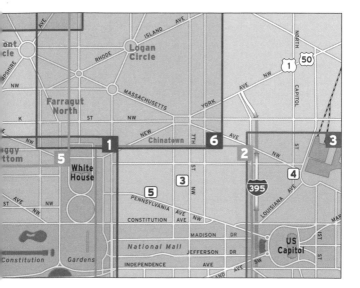

MAP 6
16

WESTERN MALL/ FOGGY BOTTOM

The western part of the Mall is a rite of passage for tourists, school groups, and history buffs. The Washington Monument marks the eastern edge of this memorial-heavy area, where tributes to Abraham Lincoln and the veterans of World War II, Korea, and Vietnam each take their place around the 2,000-foot-long Reflecting Pool. Farther south, by the Tidal Basin, are the Franklin Delano Roosevelt Memorial and the Thomas Jefferson Memorial. Springtime is *sakura* season, and the expanse brightens with lush pink cherry blossoms. This is Washington at its best and most beautiful, combining aesthetic appeal with a strong sense of history.

To the north, Foggy Bottom is the rare neighborhood where college students and upscale Washingtonians peacefully coexist. The John F. Kennedy Center for the Performing Arts and posh Watergate Complex hug the edge of the Potomac, and these blocks are also George Washington University's unofficial campus. Classroom buildings are interspersed with well-kept townhouses. However, the sleepy neighborhood isn't always serene: the White House, World Bank, and International Monetary Fund are also nearby, so protestors know the area well.

MAP 1 WESTERN MALL/FOGGY BOTTOM

MAP 1 | WESTERN MALL/FOGGY BOTTOM

LINCOLN MEMORIAL

Even if it's your first time, walking up the steps of the Lincoln Memorial feels familiar. That's probably because its image is imprinted on every U.S. penny and $5 bill, and over the years, it has become a symbol of freedom and democracy. It was here, in 1963, that Martin Luther King Jr. addressed the nation with his famous "I Have a Dream" speech. The scene of public protests and demonstrations broadcast globally, the Lincoln Memorial is understandably the city's most-visited memorial.

Construction on this Greek temple–style structure began in 1914, and Lincoln's only surviving son attended the building's dedication in 1922. The 19-foot statue of the 16th president, designed by Daniel Chester French, is about as lifelike as marble can be, and the seated, brooding figure dominates the interior space. Surrounding it are his most famous words etched in stone: the Gettysburg Address on one wall, his second inaugural address on another. The 36 Doric columns around the exterior symbolize the states in the Union at the time of Lincoln's assassination in 1865, with their names appearing on the carved frieze above the columns. Elsewhere in the monument are the names of the 48 states in the Union when the building was completed.

Packed tour buses flock to this site daily, especially in the spring and summer. If you'd rather not share the moment with a crowd, visit at dusk or early morning. By the light of a full moon, the images in the 2,029-foot-long Reflecting Pool, directly across from the main entrance, are spectacular.

MAP 1 D2✪38   23RD ST. NW 202-619-7222
HOURS: DAILY 24 HOURS
PARK RANGER HOURS: 9:30 A.M.–MIDNIGHT

NATIONAL WORLD WAR II MEMORIAL

Honoring what Tom Brokaw has called the Greatest Generation, the National World War II Memorial opened to the public on April 29, 2004, nearly 60 years after the end of the war.

Nestled between the Washington Monument and the Lincoln Memorial on the National Mall, the site is an ambitious mix of granite and bronze, with a strong circular motif and careful attention to those who played a role

⭐ SIGHTS

LINCOLN
MEMORIAL

NATIONAL WORLD WAR II
MEMORIAL

THOMAS JEFFERSON
MEMORIAL

during the war. Two flagpoles stand at the Ceremonial Entrance on 17th Street, and the base of each bears the insignia of every branch of the armed forces that served. Along the raised walkway and steps toward the plaza are 24 bronze bas-relief panels depicting those who supported the war both at home and abroad.

The monument's centerpiece is the Memorial Plaza, which incorporates a revamped Rainbow Pool and quotes from Franklin Delano Roosevelt, Harry Truman, and Dwight Eisenhower, among others. Marking the north and south entrances to the plaza, the Atlantic and Pacific Memorial Pavilions commemorate the two theaters of war. Smaller pillars, 56 in all, encircle the plaza and represent each U.S. state and territory at the time of the conflict. A sculpted bronze rope connects the pillars and pavilions, symbolizing the unity of the nation at the time. Other details include the striking, if eerie, backlights for night viewing and the sobering Field of Stars – 4,000 gold stars on the Wall of Freedom representing the 400,000 who gave all for their country.

 MAP 1 D5 ✪ 40   17TH ST. BTWN. CONSTITUTION AND INDEPENDENCE AVES. NW 202-619-7222
HOURS: DAILY 24 HOURS
PARK RANGER HOURS: 9:30 A.M.–MIDNIGHT

THOMAS JEFFERSON MEMORIAL

Thomas Jefferson's contributions to our nation – as a statesman, spiritual leader, independent thinker, and ultimately as president – were immense. He wrote the Declaration of Independence, contributed to the drafting of the U.S. Constitution, and founded the University of Virginia. Fittingly, his memorial overlooking the Tidal Basin is arguably the most graceful and inspirational structure in Washington.

The creation of the Jefferson Memorial had a bumpy

VIETNAM VETERANS MEMORIAL   WASHINGTON MONUMENT

start. In 1934, architect John Russell Pope was hired to design the structure. Inspired by Jefferson's own neo-classical architectural tastes, Pope modeled the monument on Rome's Pantheon. However, the Commission of Fine Arts worried that the open, colonnaded structure too closely resembled the Lincoln Memorial. President Franklin D. Roosevelt was asked to intervene; he liked the design and gave his permission to proceed, and in 1939, he laid the cornerstone of the memorial.

Another four years passed before Rudolph Evans was commissioned to sculpt the imperial, bronze statue of Jefferson, which stands 19 feet tall atop a six-foot granite pedestal. Carved into the walls around the statue are excerpts from Jefferson's writings: portions of the Declaration, admonitions against slavery, and statements advocating religious freedom.

The memorial is especially breathtaking in late March and early April, when the famed cherry blossoms are in bloom. At night, energy-efficient lighting illuminates parts of the site, making the after-dark experience at the Jefferson Memorial very rewarding.

MAP 1 F5✪48   EAST BASIN DR. SW 202-619-7222
HOURS: DAILY 24 HOURS
PARK RANGER HOURS: 9:30 A.M.–MIDNIGHT

VIETNAM VETERANS MEMORIAL

Known simply as the Wall, this haunting memorial to those killed or missing in the Vietnam War is a "quiet place, meant for personal reflection and reckoning." Day and night, scores of people come to do just that, paying their respects at the black granite walls etched with more than 58,000 names.

Designed by artist Maya Ying Lin, the two walls rise from grassy earth and meet at a 10-foot peak. To quell the

controversy surrounding the starkness of the sculpture, which was seen by many as too abstract, the life-size Three Servicemen Statue, depicting young servicemen of different ethnic origins, was placed nearby in 1984, two years after the memorial's dedication. In addition, the Glenna Goodacre-designed Vietnam Women's Memorial, a bronze statue of three military women tending to a fallen soldier, was erected in 1993.

Despite the many visitors, the area around the memorial is very quiet. Many bring charcoal and tracing paper to make rubbings of the names of their loved ones; some also leave behind poignant offerings such as photographs, medals, dog tags, helmets, boots, letters, birthday cards, flowers, and toys. Veterans of the conflict keep a constant vigil to provide information and emotional support.

Beautiful in all seasons and at all times of day, the walls' highly polished surfaces reflect the trees, sky, and flags in vivid color. The scene is most ethereal at night, when city traffic on Constitution Avenue has quieted and the crowds have ebbed.

MAP 1 C3032 HENRY BACON DR. AND CONSTITUTION AVE. NW 202-619-7222 HOURS: DAILY 8 A.M.-11:45 P.M.

WASHINGTON MONUMENT

Originally conceived as an equestrian statue to honor George Washington, this monument to the Father of Our Country has become the most distinguished icon in our nation's capital.

Built of brick with a marble exterior, the monument reaches 555 feet – the world's tallest masonry structure – and weighs 90,854 tons. Construction began in 1848, but political disputes, lack of funds, and the Civil War delayed its completion until 1888. Because the quarry from which the initial marble was drawn had run out by the time construction resumed after the Civil War, there is a visible color change about a third of the way up, where the Maryland marble meets the Massachusetts marble.

Today, a 60-second elevator ride whisks visitors up to the observation platform, where eight small windows afford a spectacular view of the city. There was a time when people were permitted to walk up the 896 steps to the summit. In fact, when the elevator first opened, only men were allowed to take it since it was thought to be dangerous, and women received the dubious privilege of what is literally a monumental workout.

Free tickets for timed entry into the edifice are available at the kiosk on the Washington Monument grounds on a first-come, first-served basis. (Lines are long, and tickets tend to run out quickly, especially in the spring and summer). Reserved tickets can be ordered between 24 hours and five months in advance and will cost $1.50, plus a $.50 handling fee for each order.

MAP 1 **D6●42** CONSTITUTION AVE. AND 15TH ST. SW 202-619-7222
HOURS: DAILY 9 A.M.–4:45 P.M.

THE WHITE HOUSE

Visitors are often surprised to find the White House in the heart of Washington's downtown business district surrounded by hotels, restaurants, and museums – and not in a residential neighborhood. Yet, despite its stately Greek-revival architecture and status as a symbol of the federal government, the White House is home to the president and his family.

In 1800, the first resident, John Adams, moved in. Since then, the White House has undergone many changes reflecting the wishes of its occupants: FDR added the East Wing, Harry Truman added a second-story balcony, and Bill Clinton built a custom jogging track.

Anticipated dangers to the commander-in-chief have caused security measures to tighten over the years, and regulations governing access change frequently. Until 1928, Americans could enter the White House every day at noon to meet the president. (Herbert Hoover discontinued the practice when the crowds exceeded 1,000 visitors a day.) In 1995, after an attempted shooting, the stretch of Pennsylvania Avenue in front of the building was closed permanently to automobile traffic.

The "President's house" isn't completely off limits, though. Tours for parties of 10 or more can be requested through members

SIDE WALKS

Unless you've scheduled a tour months in advance, a visit to the White House will most likely be very short. Combine your photo-op with a trip to the nearby **Corcoran Museum of Art (p. 68),** Washington's best collection of American art.

For more American works, walk a few blocks up to the **Renwick Gallery (p. 69)** for (free) decorative arts exhibits, including a not-to-be-missed display of handmade furniture.

Afterwards, stop for a rest in **Lafayette Square Park (p. 83),** surrounded by statues and stately buildings.

Go a few steps up Connecticut Avenue for dinner at **The Bombay Club (p. 22),** where you can break from the all-American theme with a meal of Indian curries.

THE WHITE HOUSE

FRANKLIN DELANO ROOSEVELT
MEMORIAL

of Congress. (Even if you don't have a party of 10, try anyway. Sometimes different groups can be combined.) Requests may be granted six months in advance and are confirmed approximately one month prior. In the summer it's best to make arrangements a few months ahead to be safe.

MAP 1 **B5✪29** 1600 PENNSYLVANIA AVE. NW
202-456-7041 (24-HOUR INFORMATION LINE)

CONSTITUTION GARDENS
This 50-acre landscaped park bordering the Reflecting Pool is an idyllic setting for a memorial dedicated to the signers of the U.S. Constitution.

MAP 1 **D5✪41** CONSTITUTION AVE. AND 17TH ST. NW
202-619-7222

EINSTEIN MEMORIAL
This bronze sculpture captures Albert Einstein lounging on a park bench as if contemplating the wonders of the universe. Its huge size makes for a great photo-op.

MAP 1 **C3✪31** 2101 CONSTITUTION AVE. NW
202-334-2138

FRANKLIN DELANO ROOSEVELT MEMORIAL
This expansive 7.5-acre park is a magnet for tourists. The best time to enjoy the waterfalls, shade trees, and sculptures is at night, without the crowds.

MAP 1 **E4✪45** 900 OHIO DR. SW
202-619-7222

KOREAN WAR VETERANS MEMORIAL
Dedicated in 1995, this hillside memorial consists of 19 larger-than-life soldiers sculpted in stainless steel. A granite wall and Pool of Remembrance add to the dramatic setting, as does fiber-optic lighting for night viewing.

MAP 1 **D3✪39** INDEPENDENCE AVE. AND DANIEL FRENCH DR. SW
202-619-7222

MAP 2 | CENTRAL MALL/SMITHSONIAN

NATIONAL AIR AND SPACE MUSEUM

From the original 1903 Wright Brothers flyer to the *Apollo 11* command module, the National Air and Space Museum holds the world's largest collection of aircraft and spacecraft. With its original location on the Mall only able to contain 10 percent of its objects, NASM opened the Steven F. Udvar-Hazy Center in late 2003.

At the museum on the Mall – a Washington landmark since 1976 – you'll find three exhibition halls with the "firsts" of flight and more than 20 galleries, including the hands-on "How Things Fly." Check out the exhibit celebrating the flight at Kitty Hawk. There's also the Lockheed Martin IMAX Theater, whose premiere film, *To Fly,* imparts the sensation of flying in a hot air balloon, a variety of airplanes, and, finally, a spacecraft.

The Udvar-Hazy Center is the larger of the two sites, by far. Located in nearby Chantilly, Virginia, the center will eventually contain nearly 80 percent of the museum's holdings, including 200 aircraft and 135 space artifacts. Currently, the nearly three-football-field-long Aviation Hangar displays more than 80 aircraft, and the adjoining James S. McDonnell Space Hangar holds *Enterprise,* the first space shuttle.

With 10 million visitors annually, NASM is the world's most-visited museum, so crowds are always a part of the experience. (However, they tend to recede in late afternoon and during the winter months.) Admission is free, but the shuttle to the Udvar-Hazy Center will cost $7.

MAP 2 E5✪62 INDEPENDENCE AVE. AND 4TH ST. SW 202-357-2700
HOURS: DAILY 10 A.M.–5:30 P.M.

NATIONAL ARCHIVES

The National Archives and Records Administration Building first opened in 1935, but the venerable institution has since grown to include the National Archives at College Park, Maryland, as well as 19 regional record facilities and 10 Presidential libraries spread out over the United States. In Washington alone, NARA houses more than six billion pieces of paper and 11 million pictures.

The main attraction of the neoclassical National Archives building on Pennsylvania Avenue is the Rotunda for the Charters of Freedom. Reopened in 2003 after a

NATIONAL AIR AND
SPACE MUSEUM

NATIONAL ARCHIVES

NATIONAL GALLERY
OF ART

three-year renovation, this exhibition space features a new-and-improved display of the Declaration of Independence, the Constitution (all four pages, a first), and the Bill of Rights. The National Archives Experience, a continuing program, includes a Special Exhibition Gallery with document-based exhibits of current affairs.

Other spaces of interest in the National Archives are the five Public Vaults, with exhibition spaces thematically connected to the Preamble to the Constitution, and the 290-seat William G. McGowan Theater. By day the theater runs a film illustrating the relationship between public records and the democratic process. At night it becomes a showcase for documentaries, as well as a gathering place for citizens to discuss issues of the day.

MAP **2** C4**◯**49 CONSTITUTION AVE. BTWN. 7TH AND 9TH STS. NW
866-272-6272
HOURS: MON. AND WED. 8:45 A.M.–5 P.M., TUES., THURS., AND FRI. 8:45 A.M.–9 P.M., SAT. 8:45 P.M.–4:45 P.M.

NATIONAL GALLERY OF ART

The National Gallery of Art was founded by financier and art collector Andrew W. Mellon. His endowment included 121 paintings, with 21 masterpieces from the Hermitage, and his collection of 15th-century Italian sculpture. Other benefactors followed suit, and within 30 years the collection outgrew the original building, leading to the addition of another building in 1978. Today, the West and East Buildings contain collections from the Middle Ages to the present.

With a domed rotunda over a marble-colonnaded fountain, the West Building is a neoclassical masterpiece. The more than 1,000 works on permanent display include paintings by Van Gogh, Rembrandt, El Greco, da Vinci, and Vermeer. You'll also find one the world's finest Impressionist collections. In contrast, the East Building,

SIDE WALKS

After exploring the National Gallery of Art's two extensive buildings, recover from your museum hangover in the **National Gallery of Art Sculpture Garden (p. 84),** located across from the West Building.

Check out the **United States Navy Memorial (p. 12)** on your walk toward the Penn Quarter for dinner.

Sup on flavorful small plates at **Jaleo (p. 25),** D.C.'s favorite purveyor of Spanish tapas.

Take a cab to the Willard Inter-Continental where you can finish out the night with drinks at the traditional haunt of power players, **Round Robin Bar (p. 44),** the lobby bar where the term "lobbying" was invented.

designed by the architecture firm of I. M. Pei, is an ultramodern palace of glass walls and jutting angles filled with works by 20th-century masters such as Picasso, Modigliani, Matisse, Pollock, and Rothko. The art displays continue to the outside, where the Sculpture Garden spreads over two city blocks and includes items by Joan Miró, Roy Lichtenstein, and Ellsworth Kelly. Year-round café service and a central fountain make it a delightful luncheon spot.

If you're susceptible to art overload, make your first stop the West Building's Micro Gallery, where you can design a personalized tour. The gallery also offers other programs, such as film series and − running September−June − Sunday evening concerts.

MAP **2** D5**⬤54** 4TH ST. AND CONSTITUTION AVE. NW 202-737-4215
HOURS: MON.-SAT. 10 A.M.-5 P.M., SUN. 11 A.M.-6 P.M.

SMITHSONIAN INSTITUTION

Founded in 1846, the Smithsonian grew out of a bequest left by English scientist James Smithson, who specified that his money be used "to found an establishment for the increase and diffusion of knowledge." His wish was carried out. With 17 museums and galleries, among them the National Zoological Park and nine research facilities around the world containing more than 143 million artifacts, the Smithsonian is the world's largest museum complex.

The museum got its start almost 160 years ago in the turreted red sandstone building known as "the Castle." A fanciful combination of Romanesque revival and early Gothic architecture, the Castle has retained its look despite several major renovations.

The state-of-the-art information center is the requisite first stop. The center provides a 24-minute film giving an overview of the Institution, interactive computer touch-screens dispensing information in six languages, and a

SMITHSONIAN
INSTITUTION

UNITED STATES HOLOCAUST MEMORIAL MUSEUM

scale model of Washington's downtown area. Electronic
wall maps highlight popular attractions, and information
specialists are on hand to answer questions concerning
the Smithsonian's lectures, concerts, festivals, and tours.

Outside, facing Independence Avenue, is the four-acre
Enid A. Haupt Garden, named for its benefactor. The
lovely plantings, brick walkways, 19th-century lampposts,
and antique benches make it perfect for a brown-bag
lunch.

Many of the Smithsonian's most popular museums,
including the National Air and Space Museum and the
Freer and Sackler Galleries, are just steps away from the
Castle. Visit-worthy for the sheer quality and quantity
of the collections, the Smithsonian museums have the
added appeal of free admission.

MAP **2** E3**❂57** 1000 JEFFERSON DR. SW 202-633-1000
MUSEUM HOURS: DAILY 10 A.M.-5:30 P.M.
INFORMATION CENTER HOURS: DAILY 8:30 A.M.-5:30 P.M.

UNITED STATES HOLOCAUST MEMORIAL MUSEUM

Dedicated to the mandate that society must never forget
the atrocities of World War II, the U.S. Holocaust Memorial
Museum opened in 1993 and has since remained one of
the most powerful, sobering, and memorable sights in
Washington.

Designed by I. M. Pei & Partners, the five-story redbrick
and limestone building is itself a major part of the experience. Occupying two acres, the huge education and
research complex resembles a postmodern penitentiary,
with a series of watchtowers along two sides.

Upon entering the permanent exhibit, you receive a
photo identity card with personal statistics about an
actual victim of the Holocaust; periodic updates on your

BUREAU OF ENGRAVING AND PRINTING   SUPREME COURT

card eventually reveal the person's fate. Using a barrage of documentary films, tapes, and personal artifacts, the permanent exhibit covers three floors, each documenting a different time span from 1933 to 1945. The exhaustive archives allow you to track the public's increasing awareness of the tragedy through films and newspaper coverage.

Many of the graphic exhibits are profoundly disturbing and are not recommended for young children. You will not soon forget these images: a roomful of shoes of the victims, an actual train car used to shuttle prisoners to the concentration camps, a white-plaster scale model of a death camp. End your visit in the 60-foot-high Hall of Remembrance, an unadorned open space provided for contemplation and commemorative ceremonies, where you can light a candle to honor one of the Holocaust victims.

MAP 2 F1✪64   100 RAOUL WALLENBERG PL. SW 202-488-0400, 800-400-9373 (TIMED-ENTRY PASSES FOR PERMANENT EXHIBIT HALL) HOURS: DAILY 10 A.M.–5:30 P.M.

BUREAU OF ENGRAVING AND PRINTING
Inside this imposing, columned government building, blank sheets of paper are transformed into bills worth $1–100, and the tour that walks you through the process is one of the most interesting and popular in Washington.

MAP 2 F1✪65   14TH AND C STS. SW 202-874-2330

NATIONAL MALL
A green expanse bordered by the Smithsonian museums, the Capitol, and various monuments, the Mall is the city's playground, where everyone is welcome and anything goes.

MAP 2 E3✪56   BTWN. CONSTITUTION AND INDEPENDENCE AVES., THE CAPITOL AND LINCOLN MEMORIAL 202-619-7222

UNITED STATES NAVY MEMORIAL
The huge plaza features a 100-foot-diameter world map, a

statue of the *Lone Sailor,* and depictions of important events in U.S. naval history.

MAP 2 C4 ● 47   701 PENNSYLVANIA AVE. NW
202-737-2300

MAP 3 | CAPITOL HILL

SUPREME COURT

Convened for the first time in 1790, the nation's highest court led a nomadic life for 145 years. Lacking a place to call their own, the justices met in various venues around New York and Philadelphia, including in private homes and occasionally in a tavern. It wasn't until 1929 that Chief Justice William Howard Taft, the only president ever to serve on the Court, convinced Congress to allocate funds for a Supreme Court building.

Located on the grounds of a former Civil War prison, the weighty neoclassical structure was designed by architect Cass Gilbert to symbolize the importance of the independent branch of government that it houses. Two massive figures representing the Contemplation of Justice and the Authority of Law flank a broad staircase that leads up to 32 Corinthian columns. Sculpted bronze entry doors open into the Great Hall, where busts of former chief justices are set on marble pedestals.

In addition to impressive architecture, a visit to the Supreme Court can offer a chance to sit in on a session. The Court hears oral arguments at 10 A.M. Monday–Wednesday, starting the first Monday of October and continuing every two weeks until late April. (The Court then continues to sit through the end of June, issuing orders and opinions.) All told, the Court decides about 100 cases of national importance a year. Reservations are not required to hear oral arguments, which are open to the public on a first-come, first-served basis.

SIDE WALKS

After visiting the Supreme Court, spend some time at the **Folger Shakespeare Library (p. 72),** a beautiful art deco building containing numerous Shakespearean works.

Move on to the **Eastern Market (p. 54),** a bustling bazaar of food, clothes, arts, and crafts. Pick up snacks or even a quick lunch.

A few blocks away, D.C.'s best dive, **Tune Inn (p. 45),** starts serving at 8 A.M. Should you need a beer, this is an option.

Back on the Hill, make your way up to Constitution Avenue and 1st Street NW for dinner at **Charlie Palmer Steak (p. 28).**

UNITED STATES CAPITOL   UNION STATION

You can choose to stay for an entire argument or a brief visit. When the Court is not in session, the staff often presents lectures every hour 9:30 A.M.–3:30 P.M.

MAP 3 D4🌑15   1 1ST ST. NE 202-479-3211
HOURS: MON.-FRI. 9 A.M.-4:30 P.M.

UNITED STATES CAPITOL

Pierre L'Enfant described Jenkins Hill as "a pedestal waiting for a monument." With its enormous cast-iron dome, Roman pillars, and ornate fountains, the U.S. Capitol building he placed on the site certainly qualifies. Sweeping lawns and flowering gardens, designed by Frederick Law Olmsted of New York's Central Park fame, enhance the neoclassical structure's beauty.

History permeates the four-acre complex, where Congress crafts laws as it has since John Adams addressed its first session in 1800. Over the years, the Capitol has been burned (during the War of 1812), rebuilt, and restored, all the while enduring as a symbol of democracy.

Appropriately, the bronze *Statue of Freedom* tops the 285-foot dome. Inside, a Constantino Brumidi frieze around the rim re-creates 400 years of history. The *Apotheosis of Washington,* an allegorical fresco by the same artist, fills the eye of the dome, while immense oil paintings by John Trumbull depict scenes from the American Revolution. Guided tours are available by obtaining a free timed-entry pass from a kiosk located near 1st Street and Independence Avenue SW.

MAP 3 D2🌑14   BTWN. CONSTITUTION AVE., INDEPENDENCE AVE., AND 1ST
ST. 202-225-6827
HOURS: MON.-SAT. 9 A.M.-4:30 P.M.

LIBRARY OF CONGRESS
With its sweeping stairways and columned halls, the Library of Congress is visually and architecturally stunning. It's almost a footnote to say it contains the world's most comprehensive col-

STREET PERFORMERS

Buskers performing on the street are not exactly the first scene that comes to mind when thinking of a stately, monument-heavy town like Washington. But, like any major city, D.C. has its share of street performers and prophets of the surreal, and none are more familiar to local denizens than Mark Francis Nickens and Fisher Yang. Jamming at Metrorail stations, Nickens is a dreadlocked, Ibanez-sporting guitar virtuoso who has played in bands and performed solo at concerts and parties all over. And anyone who's been to Union Station during morning rush will instantly recognize the horn-blowing, hymn-slinging Fisher Yang. Armed with his John 3:16 placard and a portable yellow amp, Yang sings hymns from the center main flagpole of the grand depot, also known as the makeshift Union Church of Washington.

lection of human creativity and knowledge.

MAP 3 E4✪20 THOMAS JEFFERSON BUILDING, 101 INDEPENDENCE AVE. SE
202-707-8000

NATIONAL JAPANESE AMERICAN MEMORIAL

The inscriptions at this triangular plaza commemorate Japanese patriotism during World War II. A statue depicting two cranes bound with barbed wire symbolizes the battle to overcome prejudice.

MAP 3 C2✪11 LOUISIANA AVE. BTWN. NEW JERSEY AVE. AND D ST. NW
202-530-0015

UNION STATION

At one time the world's largest train station, Union Station, with its beaux arts–style architecture, marble floors, and high coffered ceilings, is gorgeous and practical as a destination for transit, shops, and restaurants.

MAP 3 B3✪4 50 MASSACHUSETTS AVE. NE
202-289-1908

UNITED STATES BOTANIC GARDEN CONSERVATORY

First established in 1820, the nation's oldest continually operating botanic garden boasts an old world desert, numerous varieties of orchids, and – the highlight – a tropical rainforest of towering palms and steamy pools.

MAP 3 E1✪18 100 MARYLAND AVE. SW
202-225-8333

THIRD CHURCH OF CHRIST, SCIENTIST   EMBASSY ROW

MAP 4 | GEORGETOWN

COX'S ROW

Colonel John Cox – a mayor of Georgetown – built this elegant
row of houses in 1818, and today they are the postcard view of
the neighborhood. Brick sidewalks take you back to his time.

MAP 4 E3 ✪17   3327-3339 N ST. NW

GEORGETOWN UNIVERSITY

Founded in 1789, Georgetown is not only the United States'
oldest Catholic and Jesuit University, but also one of its most
beautiful and exclusive.

MAP 4 D1 ✪10   37TH ST. AT O ST. NW
202-687-0100

OAK HILL CEMETERY

Established in 1849, this enchanting garden cemetery situated on 25 hilly acres has exceptional statuary and a James
Renwick-designed Gothic-revival chapel on its grounds. No pictures allowed on the grounds.

MAP 4 B6 ✪7   3001 R ST. NW
202-337-2835

TUDOR PLACE HISTORIC HOUSE AND GARDEN

This brick mansion has dominated its block of Georgetown
since 1816. There are special programs year-round, including the
annual Tudor Place Christmas open house.

MAP 4 C4 ✪9   1644 31ST ST. NW
202-965-0400

MAP 6 LOGAN CIRCLE/U STREET

FRANKLIN SQUARE

When Alexander Graham Bell transmitted the first wireless message from here in the 1880s, this downtown park was considered "the country." The adjoining Franklin School, the only building from that era in the square still standing, was opened in 1869.

MAP 6 F4◐43   14TH ST. AT K ST. NW

THIRD CHURCH OF CHRIST, SCIENTIST

Architecture buffs won't want to miss this striking I. M. Pei-designed church, which incorporates his characteristic geometric angles.

MAP 6 F2◐39   900 16TH ST. NW
202-833-3325

MAP 7 UPPER NORTHWEST

EMBASSY ROW

A few memorable hours can be well spent by strolling along Embassy Row. More than 50 countries are represented in this two-mile stretch of Massachusetts Avenue, along with stately private homes, a charming pocketsize park, and the city's largest mosque.

Beginning with its national flag, each embassy proudly displays its unique character. The Brazilian Embassy is an ultramodern, understated glass box. The Korean Embassy boasts a fountain featuring silver globes poised atop poles. The imposing Chancery of the Italian Embassy, on Whitehaven Street, was completed in 1999; its facade is made from stones cut to size in Italy and shipped to the United States

SIDE WALKS

Turn a drive up Embassy Row into an excursion to Washington's off-the-Mall attractions. The **United States Naval Observatory (p. 18),** home of the vice president, sits at the end of all the embassies.

The breathtaking **Washington National Cathedral (p. 18)** lies farther north on a hill. Ride elevators up to the observation gallery for city views; afterwards, admire the exterior's unique gargoyles.

Next, direct your vehicle toward the sophisticated Cleveland Park neighborhood, home of Washington's finest movie theater, the one-screen Uptown (technically, **Loews Cineplex Odeon Uptown, p. 81).**

Before or after a movie, dine on New American fare at fashionable **Ardeo (p. 36).**

WASHINGTON NATIONAL
CATHEDRAL   ARLINGTON NATIONAL CEMETERY

for installation by Italian masons. The four-acre British Embassy, considered the star of Embassy Row, is housed in a magnificent redbrick residence built in 1928. A statue of Winston Churchill stands out front, with one foot on British soil – embassy grounds are technically property of that country – and the other on U.S. soil, as a symbol of his Anglo-American descent.

Just east of Rock Creek Park is the operational mosque at the Islamic Center. Visitors are welcome but proper dress is required: arms and legs must be covered, shoes must be removed, and women must wear a head covering.

While embassies are usually open for official business only, a phone call in advance of your visit may yield different results.

MAP 7 **E5✪25** MASSACHUSETTS AVE. NW BTWN. OBSERVATORY AND DUPONT CIRCLES

KAHLIL GIBRAN MEMORIAL GARDEN
Cross a stone footbridge to this wooded oasis dedicated to the Lebanese American philosopher and poet, Kahlil Gibran. Benches inscribed with Gibran's writings surround a star-shaped pool where a bust of his likeness sits.

MAP 7 **E5✪24** 3100 BLOCK OF MASSACHUSETTS AVE. NW

UNITED STATES NAVAL OBSERVATORY
Stroll the gated perimeter for a peek at the vice president's Victorian mansion, located here since 1974, but first occupied by Walter Mondale during the Carter administration.

MAP 7 **E4✪23** 3450 MASSACHUSETTS AVE. NW
202-762-1467

WASHINGTON NATIONAL CATHEDRAL
This beautiful Episcopal church's central tower rises 676 feet above sea level and forms D.C.'s highest point. Bring binoculars to appreciate the flying buttresses' quirky gargoyles and

grotesques – and the Darth Vader that sits atop the north-west tower.

`MAP 7` C3**⊙**21 WISCONSIN AVE. AT MASSACHUSETTS AVE. NW
202-537-6200

MAP 8 | ADAMS MORGAN

NATIONAL ZOOLOGICAL PARK

The home of gorillas, giant pandas, tigers, and more, the National Zoo is a sprawling 163 acres with more than 2,700 inhabitants and 435 species.

`MAP 8` A2**⊙**1 3001 CONNECTICUT AVE. NW
202-673-4800 (INFORMATION LINE); 202-673-0127
(INFORMATION DESK)

OVERVIEW MAP

ARLINGTON NATIONAL CEMETERY

A visit to Arlington National Cemetery is an emotionally charged experience. Even if you don't personally know one of the 290,000 buried here, you'll invariably feel a lump in your throat and an overwhelming rush of patriotism. Nearly 125 funeral services are performed a week, amounting to 6,000 burials a year.

The beautifully landscaped cemetery stretches over 624 hilly acres of seemingly endless rows of white headstones. Your first stop should be the visitors center, where you can pick up maps necessary to find your way around.

One of the cemetery's most crowded sights is the gravesite of President John F. Kennedy, marked with the Eternal Flame. Another moving monument is the Tomb of the Unknowns, a grave honoring the unknown soldiers of both World Wars and the Korean War. Tomb Guard Sentinels from the 3rd U.S. Infantry, the oldest active-duty unit in the Army, stand guard here 365 days a year, and the changing of the guard should not be missed.

Other points of interest include Arlington House, the restored former home of Mary Custis and her husband, Robert E. Lee; the Women in Military Service Memorial, dedicated to the women who have served in the armed forces; a memorial commemorating the astronauts killed in the space shuttle *Challenger* and *Columbia* disasters;

and Section 27, where more than 3,800 former slaves are buried.

A network of paved roads and steps cover the cemetery's often-steep terrain, and navigating the grounds involves much walking. (Cars are permitted only for the disabled or relatives of persons buried here.) The Tourmobile, a shuttle to and from the most popular sights, provides an alternative; you can arrange a ride at the visitors center.

OVERVIEW MAP **E2** VIRGINIA SIDE OF ARLINGTON MEMORIAL BRIDGE
703-607-8000
HOURS: DAILY 8 A.M.-7 P.M. (APR.-SEPT.); DAILY 8
A.M.-5 P.M. (OCT.-MAR.)

UNITED STATES MARINE CORPS WAR MEMORIAL

Also known as the Iwo Jima Memorial, this immense sculpture—based on a Pulitzer Prize-winning photograph – honors all marines who died during military duty.

OVERVIEW MAP **D2** N. MEADE ST. AT MARSHALL DR. IN ARLINGTON, VA
703-289-2500

R RESTAURANTS

Must-try restaurant of the moment: **ZAYTINYA,** p. 27

Best spot for a proposal: **1789 RESTAURANT,** p. 31

Best celeb-spotting: **CAFÉ MILANO,** p. 29

Most local flavor: **BEN'S CHILI BOWL,** p. 35

Best desserts: **BISTRO D'OC,** p. 23

Best splurge: **MICHEL RICHARD CITRONELLE,** p. 30

Best chance to overhear political gossip:
THE CAUCUS ROOM, p. 24

Best spot for a clandestine meeting:
TRYST COFFEEHOUSE BAR AND LOUNGE, p. 41

Best view: **PERRY'S,** p. 41

Best pizza: **PIZZERIA PARADISO,** p. 34

PRICE KEY

$ ENTRÉES UNDER $10

$$ ENTRÉES BETWEEN $10 AND $20

$$$ ENTRÉES OVER $20

MAP 1 | WESTERN MALL/FOGGY BOTTOM

THE BOMBAY CLUB *BUSINESS • INDIAN $$*

The Bombay Club wins hearts and return business with its gently seasoned Indian cooking, contemporary and elegant environs, and affordable prices. Despite many competitors, the Bombay Club remains a downtown favorite for lunches, dinners, and Sunday brunches.

MAP 1 A5 R11   815 CONNECTICUT AVE. NW
202-659-3727

BREAD LINE *CAFÉ $*

Just steps from the White House, Bread Line, with its frantic pace and disorderly interior, plays host to Washington's premiere power breakfast. Spot your favorite spin doctors behind the pages of *The Washington Post* as you sip fresh orange juice and grab a quick croissant.

MAP 1 A5 R13   1751 PENNSYLVANIA AVE. NW
202-822-8900

CAFÉ ASIA *HOT SPOTS • PAN-ASIAN $$*

A sleek, curved bar, well-priced sushi, and an array of carnivore- and vegetarian-friendly Asian plates make this downtown mainstay a favorite happy hour stopover. The decibels sometimes reach rock concert levels, but the young, carefree crowd doesn't seem to mind.

MAP 1 A5 R8   1720 I ST. NW
202-659-2696

EQUINOX *HOT SPOTS • AMERICAN $$$*

Chef and owner Todd Gray has created a unique restaurant with a front garden room that complements the dressier interior seating. Its proximity to the White House means big names lunch and dine here, enjoying inventive American cooking such as the spiced Virginia hanger steak with braised kale.

MAP 1 A5 R10   818 CONNECTICUT AVE. NW
202-331-8118

KINKEAD'S *BUSINESS • SEAFOOD $$$*

This wood-paneled power spot unveiled a fresh look in February 2004 with a new kitchen and swankier mood lighting. Choose between comforting favorites like lobster pie and zesty fish stew from the updated seafood menu, and the Ipswich clams, still an establishment favorite, are a must try.

MAP 1 A4 R6   2000 PENNSYLVANIA AVE. NW
202-296-7700

NECTAR *BUSINESS • NEW AMERICAN $$$*

Cozy and simple, Nectar is the rare restaurant that manages to combine neighborhood friendliness with urban elegance. A good bet for pre-Kennedy Center dining, the ever-changing menu offers progressive New American cuisine that is as dazzling as any theater performance. Try the luscious pheasant or crab with melon and avocado.

MAP 1 A2 R2   824 NEW HAMPSHIRE AVE. NW
202-298-8085

EQUINOX   NECTAR

ROOF TERRACE RESTAURANT & BAR
BUSINESS • NEW AMERICAN $$$

Inside the Kennedy Center, this glam restaurant affords its patrons a dazzling view of the Potomac River. The staid chandeliers have been replaced with shiny glass columns and the modern American menu has been kicked up a notch, with short ribs, duck breast, and tasty crab cakes.

MAP 1 B1 ℝ 17   KENNEDY CENTER, 2700 F ST. NW
202-416-8555

MAP 2 CENTRAL MALL/SMITHSONIAN

ANDALE   *BUSINESS • MEXICAN* $$

Chef Alison Swope's survey of contemporary Mexican cuisine, featuring plump empanadas, hand-made tortillas, and bubbly *queso fundido*, is a favorite of pre-theater diners. Half-priced wine on Monday nights draws a large, boisterous crowd. On other evenings, the restaurant is soothingly quiet.

MAP 2 C4 ℝ 46   401 7TH ST. NW
202-783-3133

BISTRO D'OC   *ROMANTIC • FRENCH AND AMERICAN* $$

Although this cozy Gallic bistro offers a popular three-course pre-theater menu, its friendly service encourages diners to linger. The French and American fare is reliable, but the desserts are the main attraction. Sample the indulgent crepes, oozing with lemon and butter, or order the hot, crispy *steak frites* as your after-dinner treat – they're that good.

MAP 2 B3 ℝ 25   518 10TH ST. NW
202-393-5444

BUTTERFIELD 9   *BUSINESS • NEW AMERICAN* $$$

Inspired by a Hollywood classic, Butterfield 9 looks like an edgy 1940s movie set, the perfect backdrop for its contemporary, fanciful, and often changing American dishes, such as herb-crusted rack of lamb, ahi tuna, and jumbo lump crab. Sleek, chic Washingtonians socialize at the bar.

MAP 2 B1 ℝ 9   600 14TH ST. NW
202-289-8810

BISTRO D'OC

DISTRICT CHOPHOUSE & BREWERY

CAFE ATLANTICO *HOT SPOTS • NUEVO LATINO* $$

Topping the favorites list of most D.C. gourmands, Cafe Atlantico is a lively tri-level restaurant serving unbeatable Latin-tinged fare. Addictive guacamole and a luscious dim sum–style brunch, featuring small plates like seared watermelon and scallops in orange oil, draw well-heeled crowds steered by suave servers ready with recommendations.

MAP 2 C4 R43   405 8TH ST. NW
202-393-0812

CAPITAL Q *QUICK BITES • BARBECUE* $

This no-frills barbecue shack in the heart of Chinatown is a favorite of starving students and swank politicans alike. Paper plates, paper napkins, and the tangiest barbecue sauce this side of Texas turns skeptics into regulars on the first bite.

MAP 2 A4 R5   707 H ST. NW
202-347-8396

THE CAUCUS ROOM *BUSINESS • AMERICAN* $$$

D.C. power brokers and other highbrows cozy up to the elegant bar at the posh Caucus Room. Pampered patrons enjoy steak or Maryland crab cakes with a selection from the wine list, but they save room for the kitchen's lavish desserts, such as the coconut cake.

MAP 2 C4 R42   401 9TH ST. NW
202-393-1300

CEIBA *BUSINESS • LATIN AMERICAN* $$$

Latin American cuisine, intoxicating drinks, and a lively open kitchen have kept Ceiba bustling since it opened its doors in September 2003. A tangy array of ceviches, fiery duck empanadas, and tender braised pork offer an introduction to the flavors of Brazil, Cuba, Peru, and the Yucatán.

MAP 2 A1 R2   701 14TH ST. NW
202-393-3983

DISTRICT CHOPHOUSE & BREWERY *AFTER HOURS • AMERICAN* $$

A classic American pub with its own on-site brewing vats, this eatery welcomes cigar smokers and pool players. Lunchtimes buzz with Hill folk who come for onion rings, juicy burgers, or the house's own

brown ale onion soup. Dinners attract a theater and MCI Center crowd.

MAP **2** B4 **R** 31   509 7TH ST. NW
202-347-3434

ELLA'S WOOD FIRED PIZZA   *QUICK BITES • PIZZA $$*

Don't let the staid office facade fool you — Ella's is one of the finest pizzerias in town. Tourists and locals choose from a laundry list of delicious pies topped with everything from pine nuts to shrimp. A fine array of salads, pastas, and a respectable antipasto platter rounds out the menu.

MAP **2** B4 **R** 28   9TH ST. NW BTWN. F AND G STS. NW
202-638-3434

FULL KEE   *AFTER HOURS • CHINESE $*

Soup pots simmer alongside hanging ducks in the window of this Chinatown eatery that's open till 1 A.M. on weekends. If you're feeling bold, ask the chef to prepare his favorite, though you can't go wrong with Hong Kong Noodles. Be forewarned: the specials are written in Chinese.

MAP **2** A5 **R** 7   509 H ST. NW
202-371-2233

GINGER COVE   *HOT SPOTS • CARIBBEAN $$$*

Whether you dine in the clubby upper level or downstairs in the splashy dining room, Ginger's tropical atmosphere and unmatched Caribbean cuisine won't disappoint. Tender shark, crab fritters, and mango duck are well paired with exotic cocktails.

MAP **2** B4 **R** 32   822 E ST. NW
202-248-6007

JALEO   *HOT SPOTS • SPANISH $$*

Still the most popular source for Spanish tapas in D.C., this corner eatery delights all comers with its tasteful meals and lively ambience. Chicken, mussels, sweet peppers, and potatoes are transformed into a variety of savory hot and cold dishes that pair well with crusty breads and an abundant wine selection.

MAP **2** B4 **R** 33   480 7TH ST. NW
202-628-7949

MATCHBOX   *QUICK BITES • PIZZA $$*

No bigger than its namesake, this loud New York-style pizzeria doles out crisp pies, blistered to perfection in a hand-made 900-degree oven. If pizza isn't your thing, a full menu of American favorites also awaits. You can't go wrong with tasty mini-burgers and a frosty beer.

MAP **2** A4 **R** 4   713 H ST. NW
202-289-4441

MINIBAR AT CAFE ATLANTICO   *HOT SPOTS • NUEVO LATINO $$$*

At this six-person counter within Cafe Atlantico, an innovative prix-fixe tasting menu takes guests on a culinary roller coaster. Brace yourself for some unusual combos. With dishes like Altoids crumbled over fish, this isn't for the faint of heart.

MAP **2** C4 **R** 44   405 8TH ST. NW
202-393-0812 (SPECIFY MINIBAR WHEN MAKING
RESERVATIONS)

PENN QUARTER

Until recently, Penn Quarter — the wedge of space between Chinatown and Pennsylvania Avenue — was a crumbling wasteland of boarded-up buildings. Today it's the hippest neighborhood in town. The area has enjoyed a gigantic restaurant boom, with pioneering tapas hot spots **Jaleo (p. 25)** and **Zaytinya (p. 27)** leading the charge. Flashy **Rosa Mexicano (p. 26),** pizza palaces **Matchbox (p. 25)** and **Ella's Wood Fired Pizza (p. 25),** Caribbean showplace **Ginger Cove (p. 25),** and a lively assortment of bars and nightclubs all call the neighborhood home. Within walking distance of many of the city's theaters, as well as the MCI Center, Penn Quarter has cornered the market on D.C. dining.

THE OCEANAIRE SEAFOOD ROOM *BUSINESS • SEAFOOD $$$*
Evocative of the 1930s, this luxury seafood restaurant believes that more is more, and features the freshest catches served in mammoth portions. D.C. power players and city folk come for the fine service and first-rate dishes, including fresh oysters, grilled fish, seafood soups, and heavenly key lime pie.

MAP 2 B2 Ⓡ 21 1201 F ST. NW
202-347-2277

OLD EBBITT GRILL *AFTER HOURS • AMERICAN $$*
From its breakfast pancakes to its dinnertime lamb steaks and pork chops, the Old Ebbitt serves up abundant American fare, making this buzzing place one of D.C.'s favorite haunts. Finding seating can be a challenge, even in the oyster bar, where fresh bivalves are brought in daily.

MAP 2 A1 Ⓡ 1 675 15TH ST. NW
202-347-4800

RED SAGE *BUSINESS • SOUTHWESTERN $$$*
Its casual upstairs café elevates Southwestern cooking to new heights, with flavor-packed chilis and colorful entrées. In the dressier downstairs grill, dramatic presentations of duck, tuna, lamb, and chicken blend the sunny flavors of the Mediterranean and American West, while vying for center stage with fanciful cowboy decor.

MAP 2 B1 Ⓡ 10 605 14TH ST. NW
202-638-4444

ROSA MEXICANO *HOT SPOTS • MEXICAN $$*
This new-in-2003 Manhattan import is larger than life — the guacamole is mashed tableside with flair and the frosty drinks are served in gigantic glasses. More showplace than serious dining spot, Rosa is worth visiting for the famous pomegranate margaritas alone.

MAP 2 B5 Ⓡ 37 575 F ST. NW
202-783-5522

RED SAGE   ZAYTINYA

TENPENH *BUSINESS • PAN-ASIAN* $$$
Executive chef Jeff Tunks masterminded the clever Pan-Asian menu,
culling the best curries, grills, stir-fries, and steamed dishes from
Thai, Indonesian, Filipino, and Vietnamese kitchens and giving them
his own creative twist. Even desserts fuse East and West in this
imaginative and exotic eatery.

MAP **2** C3 **Ⓡ 41** 1001 PENNSYLVANIA AVE. NW
202-393-4500

TONY CHENG'S MONGOLIAN/SEAFOOD RESTAURANT
HOT SPOTS • CHINESE $$
Gaudy and cavernous, Tony Cheng's offers two floors of dining. The
Mongolian restaurant downstairs invites guests to mix and match
meats, veggies, and sauces in a tasty stir-fry; upstairs plays host to
Hong Kong-style dim sum, as well as an array of Cantonese, Hunan,
and Szechwan specialties.

MAP **2** A5 **Ⓡ 6** 619 H ST. NW
202-371-8669

TOSCA *BUSINESS • ITALIAN* $$$
Northern Italian delicacies, served either à la carte or as a tasting
menu, are the specialty here. The dining room resembles an airport
lounge, and dishes such as the crabmeat lasagna with creamy sea
urchin sauce will make your taste buds take flight.

MAP **2** B3 **Ⓡ 23** 1112 F ST. NW
202-367-1990

THE WILLARD ROOM *BUSINESS • NEW AMERICAN* $$$
Opulent and stately, the Willard Room hosts business and political
players from breakfast through dinner. This classic restaurant caters
to foreign and national dignitaries who splurge on the seasonally
changing New American menu with items like Dover sole, beef ten-
derloin, and lobster.

MAP **2** B1 **Ⓡ 14** 1401 PENNSYLVANIA AVE. NW
202-628-9100

ZAYTINYA *HOT SPOTS • MEDITERRANEAN* $$
Crowds flock to this stylish mecca of Greek and Turkish meze, a gift
from Jaleo-mastermind chef Jose Andres. Though the no-reserva-
tions-after-6:30 P.M. policy ensures that you'll spend time at the bar,

a nibble of the light-as-air apricot fritters make the wait – and the scattered service – worthwhile.

MAP 2 A4 R3 701 9TH ST. NW
202-638-0800

MAP 3 | CAPITOL HILL

BISTRO BIS *BUSINESS • FRENCH* $$$
Bistro Bis stars super-chef Jeffrey Buben, who takes classic French fare and gives it an American nudge. Whether lounging at its zinc bar or brunching on its patio, you can celebrate such dishes as the classic signature duck confit or freshly made breakfast pastries with eggs Florentine.

MAP 3 B2 R2 HOTEL GEORGE, 15 E ST. NW
202-661-2700

CHARLIE PALMER STEAK *BUSINESS • AMERICAN* $$$
With a rooftop terrace that affords amazing Capitol views, this flashy meat monument is another jewel in chef Charlie Palmer's crown. The steaks are impossibly thick, and surf is given just as much attention as turf (try the Chesapeake blue crab).

MAP 3 C1 R9 101 CONSTITUTION AVE. NW
202-547-8100

IL RADICCHIO *ROMANTIC • ITALIAN* $$
This casual eatery, created by Roberto Donna, looks like an Italian grotto and often overflows with young crowds. Main attractions are the pizzas and spaghetti, but patrons also splurge on traditional fare like marinated lamb steak or cold veal with tuna.

MAP 3 E4 R24 223 PENNSYLVANIA AVE. SE
202-547-5114

LA COLLINE *BUSINESS • FRENCH* $$$
This understated French restaurant dishes up authentic, conventional French cooking, such as bouillabaisse and rack of lamb, to a loyal following. Located on the ground floor of an office building, it may lack romance, but its menu attracts folk from both sides of the congressional aisle.

MAP 3 B2 R3 400 N. CAPITOL ST. NW
202-737-0400

MONTMARTRE *ROMANTIC • FRENCH* $$
Montmarte offers a touch of the Left Bank in the bohemian Eastern Market. The rich French dishes, like the braised rabbit leg on a bed of creamy pasta, draw artists, families, and even the occasional politician; in the summer months, the patio is refreshing after a morning of haggling with market vendors.

MAP 3 F6 R38 327 7TH ST. SE
202-544-1244

TWO QUAIL *ROMANTIC • AMERICAN* $$$
Often voted one of D.C.'s most romantic restaurants, Two Quail

MONTMARTRE

XANDO COSÍ

resembles a Victorian attic crammed with nostalgia and charm. Located in a townhouse near Union Station, it showcases a slightly eccentric menu, including seafood tossed in macadamia cream and two quail stuffed with raspberries.

MAP 3 C4 **R** 13 320 MASSACHUSETTS AVE. NE
202-543-8030

THE WHITE TIGER RESTAURANT   *ROMANTIC • INDIAN $$*
Symbolic of the British raj, the White Tiger brings exceptional Indian cooking to D.C. The setting is romantic and beautiful, especially the alfresco terrace. The staff glide silently, serving up selections of seafood and lamb culled from the best of Indian regional cooking.

MAP 3 C4 **R** 12 301 MASSACHUSETTS AVE. NE
202-546-5900

XANDO COSÍ   *QUICK BITES • SANDWICHES $*
A stone's throw away from the Capitol, this sidewalk café is a popular gathering place for Hill staffers. The menu includes sandwiches and salads – perfect for when you're on the run – and the house specialty, make-your-own s'mores.

MAP 3 E4 **R** 27 301 PENNSYLVANIA AVE. SE
202-546-3345

MAP 4 GEORGETOWN

BISTRO FRANCAIS   *AFTER HOURS • FRENCH $$$*
With a little imagination, you may think you've landed on Paris's Left Bank. Instead, you're at this mid-Georgetown French bistro, spooning into a bowl of cheese-encrusted onion soup. A popular hangout for D.C. denizens, Bistro Francais stays open into the wee hours.

MAP 4 E5 **R** 33 3124-3128 M ST. NW
202-338-3830

CAFÉ MILANO   *AFTER HOURS • ITALIAN $$*
Frequented by journalists, politicians, and entertainers, Café Milano offers designer food for designer people. Make sure to bring plastic and stick with what's safe on the Northern Italian menu – usually

pizza and salad. Celeb-sightings on the glamorous outdoor patio sometimes compensate for the iffy cuisine.

MAP 4 E4 **R 22** 3251 PROSPECT ST. NW
202-333-6183

CLYDE'S OF GEORGETOWN *AFTER HOURS • AMERICAN* $$
The local chain's original site opened here in 1963, and helped popularize upscale pub food. Revamped, the G'town location is always crowded with folks in for brews, burgers, and the signature chili (Elizabeth Taylor apparently used to have it air-shipped).

MAP 4 E4 **R 27** 3236 M ST. NW
202-333-9180

MICHEL RICHARD CITRONELLE *BUSINESS • FRENCH* $$$
Culinary genius Michel Richard, whose California-French creations are whimsical and unpredictable, presides over this Latham Hotel restaurant. Inspired by the marketplace, Richard invents new dishes each day. The menu offers two prix-fixe options only, but both are gastronomic treats.

MAP 4 E5 **R 37** THE LATHAM HOTEL, 3000 M ST. NW
202-625-2150

MORTON'S OF CHICAGO *BUSINESS • AMERICAN* $$$
One of several Morton's in the D.C. area, this dinner-only destination is set in historic Georgetown and surrounded by shops, attracting a bustling crowd of locals and tourists. The chain's formula is simple: clubby surroundings, impeccable service, top-grade beef, and mammoth meals.

MAP 4 E4 **R 21** 3251 PROSPECT ST. NW
202-342-6258

NEYLA *ROMANTIC • MIDDLE EASTERN* $$
Unabashedly seductive, this Mediterranean grill is a swirl of opulent colors and fabrics. Even more alluring, the menu offers grilled kabobs, jumbo prawns, mounds of fresh bread, and platters of Lebanese *fattoush,* tabbouleh, and kibbe. Save room for hot tea and a creamy Lebanese *ashta* pudding.

MAP 4 E4 **R 20** 3206 N ST. NW
202-333-6353

PÂTISSERIE POUPON *CAFÉ • FRENCH* $
The incredible pastries, beautiful marzipan confections, and creative salads at Pâtisserie Poupon are the extras; the real reason to come here is for the best cup of French roast this side of the Atlantic.

MAP 4 B3 **R 4** 1645 WISCONSIN AVE. NW
202-342-3248

PEACOCK CAFÉ *CAFÉ* $$
A youthful crowd hangs out at this unpretentious yet chic café for endless cups of coffee. Enjoy a libation with a selection from the menu of salads, sandwiches, and vegetarian plates. Weekend brunches are almost obligatory if you are in the neighborhood.

MAP 4 E4 **R 23** 3251 PROSPECT ST. NW
202-625-2740

PÂTISSERIE POUPON   SEA CATCH RESTAURANT & RAW BAR

SEA CATCH RESTAURANT & RAW BAR *ROMANTIC • SEAFOOD* $$$
The raw bar gleams with shellfish on ice, and the dining room holds huge parties of seafood lovers, but the best seat in the house is on the terrace, where diners look out over the C&O Canal while delighting in the restaurant's crab cakes, lobsters, and mahimahi.

MAP 4 F5 **R47** 1054 31ST ST. NW
202-337-8855

SEASONS *BUSINESS • AMERICAN* $$$
Situated in a fashionable Georgetown hotel, this posh restaurant defines contemporary American sophistication. Lush garden greenery complements such extravagant offerings as lamb rack with braised shank and crab cakes. Breakfasts balance the healthful with the decadent – Birchermuseli versus buttermilk pancakes – and lunches and dinners follow suit.

MAP 4 E6 **R43** THE FOUR SEASONS HOTEL, 2800 PENNSYLVANIA AVE. NW
202-342-0444

1789 RESTAURANT *ROMANTIC • AMERICAN* $$$
Set in a Federal-style townhouse, this renowned restaurant showcases the cooking of much-praised Ris Lacoste, who specializes in making American dishes burst with flavor. The menu changes daily, but keep an eye out for the thick pork chops and the oyster bisque.

MAP 4 E2 **R14** 1226 36TH ST. NW
202-965-1789

MAP 5 | DUPONT CIRCLE

AL TIRAMISU *ROMANTIC • ITALIAN* $$$
This Dupont Circle hideaway serves up scrumptious Italian favorites – black truffles, imported *branzino,* and duck with balsamic vinegar and honey sauce, for example – in cozy booths are perfect for a romantic tryst. Beware: the luscious specials are sure to induce sticker-shock.

MAP 5 B4 **R20** 2014 P ST. NW
202-467-4466

ASIA NORA *ROMANTIC • PAN-ASIAN $$$*

With her upscale, certified organic Asian cuisine, celeb executive chef Nora Pouillon gives an Eastern twist to fresh and fabulous ingredients. The bewitching appeal of dishes like jasmine-smoked duck breast is marvelously complemented by the setting: elaborate wood carvings, artful high back chairs, and hanging market baskets.

MAP 5 D3 **R 43** 2213 M ST. NW
202-797-4860

DISH *HOT SPOTS • AMERICAN $$*

Dish, at the homey River Inn, is a whimsical tribute to American cooking. Everything here, from the classic meatloaf to the brassy BLT, tastes like something Mom used to make, only better. In the winter enjoy dinner by the roaring fireplace.

MAP 5 E2 **R 59** THE RIVER INN, 924 25TH ST. NW
202-338-8707

FAMOUS LUIGI'S *ROMANTIC • ITALIAN $$*

Red-checkered tablecloths, free-flowing wine, and a strolling flower salesman — Luigi's is straight out of *The Godfather*. Dine on hearty portions of garlicky red-sauce fare either inside the dark, noisy dining room or on the roomier glass-encased porch. On busy weekend nights, takeout pizza and pasta is the way to go.

MAP 5 D5 **R 50** 1132 19TH ST. NW
202-331-7574

GALILEO *BUSINESS • ITALIAN $$$*

Always one of Washington's hottest reservations, Galileo draws politicos, power couples, and expense-account types with fine northern Italian cuisine and a formal dining atmosphere. Top-flight servers bring out delicious and unusual signatures such as braised octopus and baby goat. The lunch-only bar menu offers the same quality cuisine for bargain prices.

MAP 5 D4 **R 47** 1110 21ST ST. NW
202-293-7191

JOHNNY'S HALF SHELL *ROMANTIC • SEAFOOD $$*

In its narrow digs, Johnny's Half Shell dishes out a frequently updated menu of marvelous seafood, including shrimp and grits, grilled squid, and little necks. The elegant simplicity of its offerings match the high-class surroundings — marble topped bar, tiled floor, and white-jacketed waitstaff.

MAP 5 B4 **R 21** 2002 P ST. NW
202-296-2021

KAZ SUSHI BISTRO *BUSINESS • SUSHI $$*

Renowned sushi chef Kaz Okochi tackles traditional sushi with a creative hand, often pairing the best of East and West. Beyond sushi, the menu presents several grilled specialties and artful bento boxes of tempura, rice, and meat. The cool, jade Asian décor sets a lovely scene.

MAP 5 E5 **R 61** 1915 I ST. NW
202-530-5500

KRAMERBOOKS & AFTERWORDS *AFTER HOURS • AMERICAN $$*

This bookstore/café is better for browsing than grazing, but it's still

PIZZA

For a city swarming with students and interns, Washington has long lacked decent pizza parlors. But no more. An explosion of delicious spots for New York–style and Neapolitan pies has created options that are cheap enough for bargain-seekers, yet chic enough to feel like a night out. **Matchbox (p. 25), Ella's Wood Fired Pizza (p. 25),** and **2 Amys (p. 38)** have attracted loyal followers with their thin, crisp pies. Meanwhile, **Pizzeria Paradiso (p. 34),** a mainstay in Dupont Circle for years, has branched out to a Georgetown location. Roomier than the original, it's one of the rare Georgetown restaurants that is both cheap and delicious.

a big draw for the black-turtleneck crowd. Discuss Kafka and capitalism with your waiter, or start that novel you always meant to write while lingering over gigantic veggie omelettes.

MAP **5** B5 ℝ **24** 1517 CONNECTICUT AVE. NW
202-387-1400

MARCEL'S   *ROMANTIC • FLEMISH* $$$
Chef/owner Robert Weidmaier draws on his Belgian heritage and works culinary magic in Marcel's open kitchen. Enjoy the tasteful yet casual environs while sampling the seasonal menu, studded with the likes of Coquilles St. Jacques, goat cheese terrine, and crisped soft-shell crabs.

MAP **5** D2 ℝ **41** 2401 PENNSYLVANIA AVE. NW
202-296-1166

MEIWAH   *BUSINESS • CHINESE* $$
Meiwah is a reliable source for standbys like Szechwan beef and orange chicken, all served at prices designed to encourage sharing. The hushed semi-private room upstairs is perfect for a group reunion, while the lower level offers a prime spot for people-watching. Takeout is also a popular after-work option.

MAP **5** D4 ℝ **46** 1200 NEW HAMPSHIRE AVE. NW
202-833-2888

MELROSE   *BUSINESS • NEW AMERICAN* $$$
With its floor-to-ceiling windows, marble foyer, and mint-hued walls, Melrose offers comfortable elegance and captivating New American fare. The dining room is bathed in sunlight, while the patio fountain drowns the sounds of the street. Don't miss the chocolate bread pudding.

MAP **5** D3 ℝ **42** PARK HYATT HOTEL, 1201 24TH ST. NW
202-955-3899

OBELISK   *ROMANTIC • ITALIAN* $$$
This is one of the city's finest purveyors of Italian countryside cook-

OBELISK   RAKU

ing. Delicious seasonal ingredients and a dedicated staff give the simple dining room a familial vibe. The five-course, set-priced menu lures repeat customers, both young and old.

MAP 5 B4 ⓡ17   2029 P ST. NW
202-872-1180

PESCE   *HOT SPOTS • SEAFOOD* $$$

D.C.'s top toques earned their stripes at this small, noisy restaurant off Dupont Circle. Despite the high turnover in the kitchen, this seafood standout turns out consistently high-quality fish dishes in its minimalist dining room filled with neighborhood scenesters and dating twentysomethings.

MAP 5 B4 ⓡ19   2016 P ST. NW
202-466-3474

PIZZERIA PARADISO   *QUICK BITES • PIZZA* $$

The line out the door at the Dupont branch is testimony to the unflagging popularity of the city's most famous pizzeria, which also offers tasty panini sandwiches and salads. For a more leisurely evening out, visit the roomier Georgetown outpost (3282 M St. NW; 202-337-1245), its gustatory equal.

MAP 5 B4 ⓡ16   2029 P ST. NW
202-223-1245

PRIME RIB   *BUSINESS • AMERICAN* $$$

The jacket and tie requirement sets a standard, when "anything goes" is the fashion nearly everywhere else. From the leopard skin rug and the leather booths to the tuxedoed waitstaff serving D.C.'s best beef, Prime Rib is unabashed indulgence.

MAP 5 E4 ⓡ60   2020 K ST. NW
202-466-8811

RAKU   *QUICK BITES • PAN-ASIAN* $

The New Wave menu skips across Asia for inspiration, enticing Gen X diners with excellent renditions of noodle soup, satays, wontons, and sushi. Although the service is often sluggish, the large specialty drinks and the superb see-and-be-seen outdoor patio more than make up for it.

MAP 5 A5 ⓡ12   1900 Q ST. NW
202-265-7258

SETTE OSTERIA   *QUICK BITES • PIZZA* $$
Strollers and cell phones are the popular accessories at this yuppie
Nouveau Italian *osteria*. While the pastas and pizzas are passable,
they're hardly the main event: Sette's calming patio is the chicest
place to sip a glass of wine and watch Dupont denizens strut by.

MAP **5** A4 ℝ**3**   1666 CONNECTICUT AVE. NW
202-483-3070

VIDALIA   *BUSINESS • SOUTHERN* $$$
Named after an onion that's a staple in Southern cooking, subter-
ranean Vidalia complements its updated, Southern-inflected menu
with sunny walls and a sleek wine bar. The seafood dishes are better than ever, and the sides (including a tasty mac 'n' cheese with
truffles) will delight.

MAP **5** D5 ℝ**48**   1990 M ST. NW
202-659-1990

MAP 6 | LOGAN CIRCLE/U STREET

BEN'S CHILI BOWL   *AFTER HOURS • AMERICAN* $
Anchoring the edge of a once-shadowy stretch of U Street, this
mom-and-pop institution has been slinging spicy chili, hot dogs, and
other diner favorites for generations. Place your order at the counter and take a seat next to hungry locals, partying college students,
and bewildered tourists.

MAP **6** A4 ℝ**7**   1213 U ST. NW
202-667-0909

CAFÉ LUNA   *QUICK BITES • AMERICAN* $
Luna is a fun, no-frills spot for good, cheap pizza and pasta. The
decor is limited to shards of mirror on one wall and chalkboard lists
of specials on the other – quick food is definitely the focus here.
Vegetarian and low-fat dishes abound.

MAP **6** C2 ℝ**20**   1633 P ST. NW
202-387-4005

GEORGIA BROWN'S   *BUSINESS • SOUTHERN* $$$
This lively joint serves up the best of Southern Low Country cooking,
where Hoppin' John and collard greens share the stage with surf 'n'
turf. Dine under a tangle of metal kudzu, which floats from the ceiling, and expect a boisterous crowd.

MAP **6** F3 ℝ**41**   950 15TH ST. NW
202-393-4499

KUNA   *ROMANTIC • ITALIAN* $
Generous portions of delicious rustic Italian pastas aren't all that
distinguish Kuna from the pack: Servers treat the youngish crowd
like family, and the cozy rooms, flickering candlelight, and gratis
wine tastings keep the vibe low key.

MAP **6** A4 ℝ**5**   1324 U ST. NW
202-797-7908

KUNA   CAFÉ DELUXE

LOVE CAFE *CAFÉ* $
You'll feel like you wandered onto the *Friends* set at this cozy sandwich shop, an extension of the popular Cakelove bakery across the street. Students with laptops take up residence on the cushy couches; couples linger over coffee and sandwiches. Delicious Cakelove pastries are also available.

MAP 6 A3 ® 3   1501 U ST. NW
202-265-9800

OLIVES *BUSINESS • MEDITERRANEAN* $$$
With its center-stage kitchen and chef's table, two levels of dining, and spectacular wine cellar, Todd English's D.C. Olives branch brings life to an otherwise quiet section near 16th Street. The Mediterranean-meets-New England menu offers playful food to match the high-energy atmosphere.

MAP 6 F2 ® 38   1600 K ST. NW
202-452-1866

SUSHI TARO *HOT SPOTS • SUSHI* $$$
Sit at Washington's longest sushi bar and watch a small army of chefs slice and sculpt the freshest of fish. Or dine on mats at one of the low, traditional tables, where you can try the *kaiseki*, a formal 10-course menu highlighting a variety of Japanese cuisine.

MAP 6 C2 ® 19   1503 17TH ST. NW
202-462-8999

MAP 7 | UPPER NORTHWEST

ARDEO *BUSINESS • NEW AMERICAN* $$
Cleveland Park's brashly hip New American hot spot serves up a seafood-heavy menu, featuring jerk grilled mahimahi and blue crab bisque, complemented by an opinionated, friendly staff. Small tables with stylish, wood-backed chairs fill the dining room, while mauve and sea-green booths line the walls.

MAP 7 B6 ® 19   3311 CONNECTICUT AVE. NW
202-244-6750

BUSARA *HOT SPOTS • THAI* $$

Contemporary Asian art hangs on the walls and brightens the table-
tops at this marvelous Thai restaurant. Menu highlights include traditional pad thai and curries. (Pay heed to the chili symbols, which
denote heat level.) An enclosed garden offers a relaxing alternative
to the busy interior.

MAP 7 E2 ® 22   2340 WISCONSIN AVE. NW
202-337-2340

CACTUS CANTINA *HOT SPOTS • SOUTHWESTERN* $$

The sprawling expanse of Cactus Cantina is a testament to the
popularity of Tex-Mex in D.C. Southwestern art, cowboy boots, and
old photos of Mexican cowboys greet patrons at the entrance. Locals
come back for overflowing fajita platters and ample margaritas.

MAP 7 B2 ® 13   3300 WISCONSIN AVE. NW
202-686-7222

CAFÉ DELUXE *ROMANTIC • AMERICAN* $$

Art nouveau details, from ceiling fans to thick glass partitions to
hardwood floors, accent this understated American bistro. The name
may say deluxe, but the food is blessedly simple. Both families and
young hipsters drop in for classic fare like grilled lamb chops and
reuben sandwiches.

MAP 7 B2 ® 14   3228 WISCONSIN AVE. NW
202-686-2233

FIREHOOK BAKERY AND COFFEEHOUSE *CAFÉ* $

With its beautiful exposed brick, hardwood floors, sunroof, and intimate garden patio, the Cleveland Park Firehook branch is the finest
of this small D.C. chain. Indulge in some of the city's best baked
goods, from breakfast pastries to sourdough breads.

MAP 7 A6 ® 6   3411 CONNECTICUT AVE. NW
202-362-2253

INDIQUE *HOT SPOTS • INDIAN* $$

Feast on a modern mix of Indian-style tapas and classics (think crisp
samosas, *dosas*, and fiery *vindaloos*), graciously proffered in a dramatic two-level setting, designed to resemble a personal residence.
After a potent tamarind margarita – the restaurant's signature libation – you'll feel right at home.

MAP 7 A5 ® 2   3512-3514 CONNECTICUT AVE. NW
202-244-6600

LAVANDOU *BUSINESS • FRENCH* $$

Lavandou doesn't wow crowds – it comforts them. The long-
simmered *daube de boeuf* and roasted peppers stuffed with chèvre
dissolve on the tongue. Relax and linger over the unpretentious flavors of Provence; the slow waitstaff gives you little alternative.

MAP 7 B6 ® 17   3321 CONNECTICUT AVE. NW
202-966-3002

NAM VIET PHO – 79 *QUICK BITES • VIETNAMESE* $

Forget about decor and service – just be glad all the effort went into
the menu. The selection of Vietnamese classics, from caramel pork

SPICES ASIAN RESTAURANT & SUSHI BAR   LEBANESE TAVERNA

to pho noodle soup, draws a steady crowd. One taste of the summer rolls dipped in peanut sauce and the barren walls are forgotten.

MAP 7 A6 Ⓡ 4   3419 CONNECTICUT AVE. NW
202-237-1015

PALENA   *HOT SPOTS • ITALIAN AND FRENCH*   *$$$*

White House kitchen alumni Frank Ruta and Ann Amernick dish up some of D.C.'s finest Italian- and French-influenced fare. Luxuriate in the soft, romantic setting and be swept away by stellar service. Note to the budget conscious: Check out the well-priced bar bargains.

MAP 7 A5 Ⓡ 3   3529 CONNECTICUT AVE. NW
202-537-9250

SPICES ASIAN RESTAURANT & SUSHI BAR
HOT SPOTS • PAN-ASIAN   *$$*

Pistachio- and smoke-hued walls, a blond-wood bar, and handmade chopsticks contribute to the glossy chic of this uptown eatery. Sample raw fish, or indulge in bowls of silken udon noodles in crystalline broth. Gracious service blends with creative, contemporary Pan-Asian cuisine.

MAP 7 A6 Ⓡ 8   3333-A CONNECTICUT AVE. NW
202-686-3833

2 AMYS   *QUICK BITES • PIZZA*   *$$*

Authentic, crisp Neopolitan pizza make this cheery pizza parlor a neighborhood favorite. Delectable deviled eggs with green sauce, salt-cod fritters, Marsala custard, and a sinful cheese platter are gourmet touches that are comparable to any upscale restaurant.

MAP 7 B2 Ⓡ 12   3715 MACOMB ST. NW
202-885-5700

MAP 8 | ADAMS MORGAN

BISTROT DU COIN *ROMANTIC • FRENCH $$*
"Cigarettes, cigars, oui!" reads the menu at this fuss-free Parisian
bistro. Enjoy cassoulet, *steak frites*, or chocolate mousse under the
cathedral-high ceiling. Or sidle up to the zinc bar to sip a Lillet and
brush up on your French with the expatriates.

MAP 8 F4 R 45 1738 CONNECTICUT AVE. NW
202-234-6969

CASHION'S EAT PLACE *HOT SPOTS • AMERICAN $$$*
With retro family photos dotting the wall, this upscale American res-
taurant matches its motif with old-style service. The daily-changing
menu is a melange of simply prepared food focusing on the D.C. region
and its seasons – don't miss the Potatoes Anna. Masterful martinis
await at the raised bar.

MAP 8 C5 R 12 1819 COLUMBIA RD. NW
202-797-1819

THE DINER *AFTER HOURS • AMERICAN $*
One of the few 24-hour spots in D.C., this bright, cheery space brims
with activity. Order breakfast all day or try one of the home-style
favorites: mac and cheese, meatloaf, or rosemary chicken. Fun for
the family; manna for the night owl.

MAP 8 C5 R 17 2453 18TH ST. NW
202-232-8800

LA FOURCHETTE *ROMANTIC • FRENCH $$*
Exposed brick and sunny murals decorate this cozy den of French
country cuisine. Escargot, bouillabaisse, and sweetbreads are menu
staples, graciously served from the family-run kitchen. Dine under
high ceilings in the front room or bask in the sun out back.

MAP 8 D5 R 28 2429 18TH ST. NW
202-332-3077

LAURIOL PLAZA *HOT SPOTS • MEXICAN $$*
This hangar-sized house of Spanish-Mexican cuisine pulls in crowds
every night. Three levels offer abundant sidewalk café-style seating
and a dazzling rooftop bar. The huge portions of fajitas and burritos
are as tasty as the eye-candy clientele.

MAP 8 E5 R 40 1835 18TH ST. NW
202-387-0035

LEBANESE TAVERNA *BUSINESS • MIDDLE EASTERN $$*
This bustling Middle Eastern eatery boasts a welcoming bar with two
dozen wines by the glass. Savor the aromas escaping from the open
kitchen while building an appetite for the generous portions of shish
kabob and rotisserie-roasted lamb shawarma.

MAP 8 B3 R 3 2641 CONNECTICUT AVE. NW
202-265-8681

LITTLE FOUNTAIN CAFÉ *ROMANTIC • AMERICAN $$*
The perfect romantic getaway is just steps from Adams Morgan's
busy main drag. Almost hidden, this basement bistro with low ceilings,

MESKEREM   TEAISM

oak beams, and a tiny bar has a mysterious, seductive air. Peruse
the changing menu of simple Continental cuisine with someone
special.

MAP 8 D5 R 30   2339 18TH ST. NW
202-462-8100

MANTIS   *HOT SPOTS • PAN-ASIAN*   *$*

With a sleek touch of SoHo, Mantis is a rare combination of stylish
bar and serious dining. Sip a designer martini while grazing on beef
satay, crab won tons, and other Asian nibbles. Arrive early for a
seat outside; after dark, the metallic bar is packed with twentysomethings.

MAP 8 D5 R 22   1847 COLUMBIA RD. NW
202-667-2400

MESKEREM   *HOT SPOTS • ETHIOPIAN*   *$$*

In the heart of D.C.'s Little Addis Ababa, Meskerem offers authentic
Ethiopian fare to match its alluring furnishings. Scoop up spicy
doro wat chicken with spongy *injera* bread, and sip honey wine as
you relax on cushions or carved-wood chairs. Vegetarian options
abound.

MAP 8 D5 R 25   2434 18TH ST. NW
202-462-4100

NEW HEIGHTS   *ROMANTIC • NEW AMERICAN*   *$$$*

Perched high above Rock Creek Park, this elegant treehouse is
perfect for a second date or business dinner. The seasonal New
American menu, acclaimed wine list, and solicitous staff all earn
high marks. Dinner only.

MAP 8 C3 R 7   2317 CALVERT ST. NW
202-234-4110

PASTA MIA   *HOT SPOTS • ITALIAN*   *$*

With its perennial pasta favorites served in portions likely to leave
patrons with tomorrow's lunch, this unassuming Italian eatery fills
up nightly with students, families, and hipsters. You may have to
wait for a seat at one of the checkered tablecloth tables, but it's well
worth it.

MAP 8 C5 R 10   1790 COLUMBIA RD. NW
202-328-9114

PERRY'S *HOT SPOTS • NEW AMERICAN $$*

Formerly notable more for its rooftop party scene than its cuisine, Perry's has reworked its menu to offer delicious twists on New American cooking. Sushi, once the only attraction, now competes with seasonal specials like roasted ostrich and pumpkin soup. Of course, the view from the rooftop is still as enticing as ever.

MAP 8 C5 R 11   1811 COLUMBIA RD. NW
202-234-6218

SAIGONNAIS *QUICK BITES • VIETNAMESE $*

This intimate Vietnamese restaurant, with its peach walls and blue curtains, is an ideal spot for a lingering conversation or a quick, quiet meal. Straw peasant hats hang from the ceiling above as patrons sample grilled shrimp in rice paper or five-spice chicken, dishes mild enough for all tastes.

MAP 8 D5 R 32   2307 18TH ST. NW
202-232-5300

TEAISM *CAFÉ • PAN-ASIAN $*

The tiny upstairs seating area at Teaism's R Street location, with its low ceiling, simple wooden décor, and hanging screens, offers welcome seclusion from the bustle of Dupont Circle. The menu is a colorful melange of light pan-Asian fare and more than 20 teas. Don't miss the plum soup.

MAP 8 F4 R 48   2009 R ST. NW
202-667-3827

TRYST COFFEEHOUSE BAR AND LOUNGE
QUICK BITES • SANDWICHES $

Freshly baked cookies and breakfast pastries give way in the evening to beers and bourbon shots. People-watch from one of the recliners or loveseats while munching on one of the playful sandwich selections (named after regulars).

MAP 8 C5 R 16   2459 18TH ST. NW
202-232-5500

N NIGHTLIFE

MAP 2 CENTRAL MALL/SMITHSONIAN

JOHN HARVARD'S BREW HOUSE *PUB*

A part of the Massachusetts chain, this basement pub is spacious with a high, curvy copper ceiling. The wait for a booth isn't very long early in the evening.

MAP 2 B2 N 20 1299 PENNSYLVANIA AVE. NW
202-783-2739

ROUND ROBIN BAR *BAR*

The term "lobbying" was invented in the Willard's lobby bar, a dark green, studylike room where you can imagine – or see – people waiting in the leather chairs to meet with representatives.

MAP 2 B1 N 14 WILLARD INTER-CONTINENTAL, 1401 PENNSYLVANIA AVE. NW
202-637-7348

SKY TERRACE *BAR*

Get a rooftop view of the whole city from this relaxed outdoor bar in Hotel Washington. Expect a long, but worthwhile, wait in nice weather. Summertime only.

MAP 2 B1 N 11 HOTEL WASHINGTON, 515 15TH ST. NW
202-638-5900

MAP 3 CAPITOL HILL

BULLFEATHERS *BAR*

Named after one of Teddy Roosevelt's expletives, Bullfeathers caters to Capitol Hill staffers. You may even catch sight of your representative having drinks in this large, early 1900s-style space.

MAP 3 F3 N 34 410 1ST ST. SE
202-543-5005

CAPITOL LOUNGE *PUB*

A classic bar with brass fixtures, two well-kept pool tables, and political memorabilia, this is where congressmen, lobbyists, staffers, and a slightly younger crowd flock after a busy day on the Hill.

MAP 3 E4 N 26 231 PENNSYLVANIA AVE. SE
202-547-2098

MR. HENRY'S *PUB*

This classic Hill pub has been a local favorite for decades. Catch the great Friday night jazz sessions in the upstairs bar, where Roberta Flack got her start back in the late '60s.

MAP 3 F5 N 35 601 PENNSYLVANIA AVE. SE
202-546-8412

POUR HOUSE *BAR*

Three unique floors – a German *biergarten* in the basement, a sports bar on the ground floor, and a plush lounge upstairs – make

this the Hill's most eclectic nightspot and a destination worth crossing town for.

MAP **3** E4 **Ⓝ28**   319 PENNSYLVANIA AVE. SE
202-546-1001

TUNE INN   *PUB*

Established in 1947, D.C.'s best dive starts serving beer at 8 A.M. Cheap drinks and packed tables keep company with an eclectic mix of photos and hunting trophies on the walls.

MAP **3** E4 **Ⓝ29**   331 ½ PENNSYLVANIA AVE. SE
202-543-2725

MAP **4** GEORGETOWN

BILLY MARTIN'S TAVERN   *PUB*

Georgetown's oldest pub drips with history. Once a Civil War prison and Corcoran family art gallery, it has served hearty comfort food and drinks to every U.S. president since Harry Truman.

MAP **4** E4 **Ⓝ24**   1264 WISCONSIN AVE. NW
202-333-7370

BLUEGIN   *LOUNGE/DANCE CLUB*

Cleverly tucked away from the bustle of Wisconsin Avenue, Bluegin boasts a strong roster of deejays and a chic ambience that sets it apart from Georgetown's pub-centric nightlife scene.

MAP **4** E4 **Ⓝ28**   1206 WISCONSIN AVE. NW
202-965-5555

BLUES ALLEY   *MUSIC CLUB*

A local landmark since 1965, this intimate supper club has hosted some of the greatest names in jazz, such as Dizzy Gillespie and Sarah Vaughan. Enjoy spicy Creole cuisine with the music.

MAP **4** F4 **Ⓝ46**   1073 WISCONSIN AVE. NW
202-337-4141

THE GUARDS   *PUB*

Dark with wood furnishings, this pub is all business in the early evening and collegiate late at night. In winter, toss back a few next to the crackling fire.

MAP **4** E6 **Ⓝ38**   2915 M ST. NW
202-965-2350

MIE N YU   *BAR*

Striking Asian decor – elegant hanging lanterns, gold statues of Hindu gods – sets the scene at this restaurant bar, and the outstanding wine selection will make you want to sample all night long.

MAP **4** E5 **Ⓝ30**   3125 M ST. NW
202-333-6122

MODERN   *LOUNGE*

With a geometric decor that's true to its name, this exquisite lounge

DRAGONFLY   BLACK CAT

is upscale and hip while remaining attitude-free. Despite the dress code and cover charge, it's a comfortable place to relax with friends.

MAP **4** E3 **18** 3287 M ST. NW
202-338-7027

SEQUOIA *BAR*
Sequoia's multilevel patio on the Potomac is *the* place to see and be seen on a sunny day. The waterfront views also make it a good, if pricey, place for a date.

MAP **4** F5 **51** 3000 K ST. NW
202-944-4200

MAP **5** | DUPONT CIRCLE

BIDDY MULLIGANS *BAR*
A low-key place to get a pint and talk with friends, this large hotel bar on Dupont Circle is a rare find: an Irish bar without Irish music.

MAP **5** B5 **26** JURYS WASHINGTON HOTEL, 1500 NEW HAMPSHIRE AVE. NW
202-797-0169 OR 202-483-6000

BRICKSKELLER *BAR*
Interesting beer bottles decorate the small brick rooms of this beer lover's heaven. Sit at one of the wooden tables, and choose from the global assortment of 500 brews.

MAP **5** B3 **13** 1523 22ND ST. NW
202-293-1885

CAFE CITRON *DANCE CLUB*
When the weather is warm, the weekend starts early at this three-story dance club popular with the young professional and international sets. Expect large crowds reveling to salsa and merengue Wednesday–Saturday nights.

MAP **5** C5 **32** 1343 CONNECTICUT AVE. NW
202-530-8844

DRAGONFLY *LOUNGE*
Japanime films flash on the all-white decor while gorgeous bartend-

ers pour cosmos at this ultrahip nightspot. The sushi is delectable, and there's never a cover charge.

MAP **5** C6 Ⓝ **40**   1215 CONNECTICUT AVE. NW
202-331-1775

EIGHTEENTH STREET LOUNGE *LOUNGE*
An unmarked door leads into this multistory lounge and dance club. Run by the group that owns the Eighteenth Street Lounge music label, this is the best place in town to hear hip new lounge and electronica sounds.

MAP **5** C5 Ⓝ **38**   1212 18TH ST. NW
202-466-3922

HERITAGE BRASSERIE AND LOUNGE *BAR*
Well-made martinis and tempting Indian tapas – including the popular samosas – materialize from behind the 55-foot granite bar. On weekend nights a beautiful club crowd grooves to Punjabi, salsa, and hip-hop beats.

MAP **5** C5 Ⓝ **33**   1337 CONNECTICUT AVE. NW
202-331-1414

OZIO *BAR*
This high-end martini and cigar bar sits in a neighborhood that otherwise caters to a younger crowd. Dress up and pay a cover on weekends to get into the dimly lit, ochre-colored digs.

MAP **5** C5 Ⓝ **37**   1813 M ST. NW
202-822-6000

TOWN & COUNTRY LOUNGE *BAR*
A sparse, well-dressed crowd frequents this piano lounge in the fashionable Mayflower Hotel. The elegant decor includes a marble bar, leather chairs, and wooden furnishings.

MAP **5** D6 Ⓝ **54**   RENAISSANCE MAYFLOWER HOTEL, 1127 CONNECTICUT
AVE. NW 202-347-3000

MCCXXIII *DANCE CLUB*
Spinning hip-hop, house, and international dance music, "12-23" draws a dynamic audience and hosts various theme nights. The strict dress code promotes the club's swank vibe, but exposed brick walls and candles add an arty touch.

MAP **5** C6 Ⓝ **39**   1223 CONNECTICUT AVE. NW
202-822-1800

MAP **6** | LOGAN CIRCLE/U STREET

BLACK CAT *MUSIC CLUB*
This rock-and-roll haven opens its doors seven nights a week for large crowds who come to enjoy the diverse range of buzz-worthy alternative bands and dance events.

MAP **6** B3 Ⓝ **13**   1811 14TH ST. NW
202-667-4490 (BAR); 202-667-7960 (CONCERT LINE)

U STREET MUSIC

Jazz has thrived along U Street ever since the days when Duke Ellington lived here in the early 1900s. Today, **Bohemian Caverns (p. 48)** is the largest and best-known jazz venue, but for more intimate sessions check out Twins Jazz (1344 U St. NW, 202-234-0072), Café Nema (1334 U St. NW, 202-667-3215), and **HR-57 (p. 80)**. This neighborhood also boasts D.C.'s best rock music scene. With two excellent stages, the **Black Cat (p. 47)** is the best place in town to catch rising stars. Virtually every big alternative act in recent memory, from Radiohead to the White Stripes, rocked this house before going mainstream. Locals also love The Velvet Lounge (915 U St. NW, 202-462-3213) and **DC9 (p. 48),** two smaller clubs regularly buzzing with great talent.

BOHEMIAN CAVERNS *JAZZ CLUB*
You can get supper, but music is the reason people flock to Washington's oldest jazz club. Brave souls offer jazz poetry on Open Mic Wednesdays.

MAP **6** A5 Ⓝ 8   2001 11TH ST. NW
202 299-0801

CAFÉ SAINT EX/GATE 54 *BAR*
Upstairs, Saint-Ex features a polished wooden bar and a fine menu of classic and contemporary European cuisine. Downstairs is Gate 54, a friendly hipster lounge where deejays spin a variety of genres nightly.

MAP **6** B3 Ⓝ 11   1847 14TH ST. NW
202-265-7839

CLUB CHAOS *QUEER*
An institution of the queer club scene, Chaos offers a high-energy dance club vibe and very cheap drinks. Perky drag queens serve you at the popular Sunday brunch, which attracts a mixed clientele.

MAP **6** C2 Ⓝ 17   1603 17TH ST. NW
202-232-4141

DC9 *BAR*
Super-friendly bartenders, strong drinks, and a jukebox with countless options – from Prince to the Smiths – make this a standout in the neighborhood bar set. Local and national bands and deejays perform several nights a week on the upstairs stage.

MAP **6** A5 Ⓝ 10   1940 9TH ST. NW
202-483-5000

9:30 CLUB *MUSIC CLUB*
This pantheon of punk accommodates 1,000 dancing, drinking

guests and hosts the likes of Wilco and Groove Armada. Escape to the downstairs bar to avoid the crush.

MAP 6 A5 ● 9 815 V ST. NW
202-393-0930 (CONCERT LINE)

TABARD INN *BAR*

Sip after-dinner drinks upon intimate couches around a fireplace in this bed-and-breakfast inn; you'll feel like you're a guest in a friend's beautiful townhouse.

MAP 6 D1 ● 24 1739 N ST. NW 20036
202-331-8528

TOPAZ BAR *LOUNGE*

A sleek, curvy bar is the centerpiece of this hip little hotel lounge. The signature martini, Blue Nirvana, is a tasty creation of citrus vodka and fruit liqueurs topped with champagne.

MAP 6 D1 ● 25 THE TOPAZ HOTEL, 1733 N ST. NW
202-393-3000

U-TOPIA *BAR*

Looking like a below-ground Paris jazz cave, tiny U-topia was among the first on U Street's hot nightlife scene. Great food tags along with the live jazz and blues.

MAP 6 A3 ● 4 1418 U ST. NW
202-483-7669

MAP 7 UPPER NORTHWEST

AROMA *BAR*

The creative bartenders at this swank martini bar can mix you clever drink variations, such as a metropolitan with fresh raspberries. Brightly colored modernistic furnishings make the back lounge a stylish place to relax with a group.

MAP 7 A6 ● 5 3417 CONNECTICUT AVE. NW
202-244-7995

BARDEO *WINE BAR*

A wine bar with shiny, modern décor, Bardeo offers numerous tables for intimate tête-à-têtes and a wide range of reasonably priced wines.

MAP 7 B6 ● 20 3309 CONNECTICUT AVE. NW
202-244-6550

IRELAND'S FOUR PROVINCES *PUB*

This large pub doesn't shy away from the Irish trappings: there's always Irish music, plenty of Guinness, and lines on St. Patrick's Day that go around the block.

MAP 7 A6 ● 11 3412 CONNECTICUT AVE. NW
202-244-0860

MAP 8 | ADAMS MORGAN

CHI CHA LOUNGE *LOUNGE*
Comfy velvet couches and Peruvian appetizers are the signatures of
this dimly lit lounge. The semi-regular live jazz often fills the place
up, but it's still intimate enough for conversation.

MAP 8 E6 Ⓝ41 1624 U ST. NW
202-234-8400

FELIX/SPY LOUNGE *LOUNGE*
Two identities compose this double agent of nightspots. Felix serves
up live jazz and funk with great food (try the crab cakes); Spy
Lounge has an ultrachic decor and superb specialty martinis like the
espresso-spiked Dr. No.

MAP 8 D5 Ⓝ26 2406 18TH ST. NW
202-483-3549

HABANA VILLAGE BAR AND RESTAURANT *BAR*
Wildly popular salsa lessons bring this bar to life Wednesday–
Saturday. Dark wooden walls and gorgeous Latin American hunting
masks make for a classy decor, and the sweet, bubbly mojitos are
unforgettable.

MAP 8 C5 Ⓝ13 1834 COLUMBIA RD. NW
202-462-6310

MADAM'S ORGAN *MUSIC CLUB*
Redheads get half-priced Rolling Rocks at this blues house with live
bands and Southern cooking. The motto says it all: "Where the beautiful people go to get ugly."

MAP 8 C5 Ⓝ15 2461 18TH ST. NW
202-667-5370

THE REEF *BAR*
Shimmering tropical fish tanks and a huge rooftop patio provide
loads of eye candy at this hot nightspot, and the all-draft beer selection is one of Adams Morgan's finest.

MAP 8 C5 Ⓝ18 2446 18TH ST. NW
202-518-3800

TOLEDO LOUNGE *BAR*
Decorated with red neon and anything else reminiscent of Toledo,
this is the quintessential neighborhood bar: Locals know the bar-
tender, drink cheap beer, and come to unwind after work.

MAP 8 D5 Ⓝ27 2435 18TH ST. NW
202-986-5416

SHOPS

MAP 1 | WESTERN MALL/FOGGY BOTTOM

AMERICAN INSTITUTE OF ARCHITECTS BOOKSTORE
BOOKS

Located inside the A.I.A., this sleek store sells the latest books and periodicals on architecture and design, as well as unusual gifts with an architectural focus.

MAP 1 B5 ⑤ 27   1735 NEW YORK AVE. NW
202-626-7475

TOWER RECORDS *BOOKS AND MUSIC*

Tower was one of the first music megastores to arrive in D.C. Open 'til midnight most nights, the two stories of CDs and tapes draws browsers at all hours of the day and night.

MAP 1 A3 ⑤ 3   2100 PENNSYLVANIA AVE. NW
202-331-2400 (MUSIC) OR 202-223-3900 (VIDEO)

WORLD BANK INFOSHOP *BOOKS*

A playground for policy wonks, this large bookstore in the World Bank carries not best-selling fiction, but a very specialized collection focusing on the development and economy of various nations.

MAP 1 A4 ⑤ 7   1818 H ST. NW
202-458-5454

MAP 2 | CENTRAL MALL/SMITHSONIAN

APARTMENT ZERO *GIFT AND HOME*

Step into this sleek store for everything for the modern urban apartment: retro lamps, metallic picture frames and office accessories, as well as stylish wooden furniture.

MAP 2 C4 ⑤ 45   406 7TH ST. NW
202-628-4067

ARTIFACTORY *GIFT AND HOME*

Housed in one of the city's oldest buildings, Artifactory's African and Asian textiles, masks, sculpture, and clothing range from inexpensive to exorbitant for certain museum-quality pieces.

MAP 2 C5 ⑤ 50   641 INDIANA AVE. NW
202-393-2727

CELADON SPA *BATH, BEAUTY, AND SPA*

A pristine haven in a downtown dead zone, Celadon is a serene respite for tired nine-to-fivers and visitors craving pampering; it offers everything from dreamlike pedicures to wraps and massages.

MAP 2 B2 ⑤ 22   1180 F ST. NW
202-347-3333

CHANEL BOUTIQUE AT THE WILLARD COLLECTION
CLOTHING AND SHOES

You'll find the classic line of suits, shoes, bags, and jewelry in this

AMERICAN INSTITUTE
OF ARCHITECTS
BOOKSTORE

APARTMENT ZERO

CHAPTERS: A LITERARY
BOOKSTORE

immaculate shop. This location is one of the largest Chanel boutiques in the world.

MAP **2** B1 **S** 13   1455 PENNSYLVANIA AVE. NW
202-638-5055

CHAPTERS: A LITERARY BOOKSTORE *BOOKS*
A sizable independent bookstore, Chapters has a knowledgeable staff, a great collection of fiction, and a schedule of readings with renowned authors.

MAP **2** B3 **S** 27   445 11TH ST. NW
202-737-5553

OLSSON'S BOOKS AND RECORDS *BOOKS AND MUSIC*
One in D.C.'s oldest chain of independent book and music stores, the Penn Quarter branch leans toward books on policy and analysis issues. There's also a large arts and ancient history selection.

MAP **2** B4 **S** 35   418 7TH ST. NW
202-638-7610

POLITICAL AMERICANA *GIFT AND HOME*
A small shop with a few too many generic D.C. souvenirs, Political Americana also carries treasures: one-of-a-kind historical photos, videos, and signed documents from politicians.

MAP **2** B2 **S** 16   1331 PENNSYLVANIA AVE. NW
800-333-4555

SOUVENIR STANDS *GIFT AND HOME*
Get all your inexpensive souvenirs in one swift shot at the numerous vans that litter the Mall. The standing deal for years has been three D.C. T-shirts for $10.

MAP **2** E2 **S** 55   VARIOUS LOCATIONS ON THE MALL

MAP 3 | CAPITOL HILL

ART & SOUL   *GIFTS AND HOME*
Selling contemporary wearable art, jewelry, and crafts, this sophisticated little shop is the ideal place to find a gift.

MAP 3 E4 Ⓢ 25   225 PENNSYLVANIA AVE. SE
202-548-0105

CLOTHES ENCOUNTERS OF A SECOND KIND
CLOTHING
This high-class consignment shop features only in-style and in-season clothing. They carry hand-selected classic clothes and designer-name business suits at reasonable – though not cheap – prices.

MAP 3 E6 Ⓢ 30   202 7TH ST. SE
202-546-4004

EASTERN MARKET   *SHOPPING DISTRICTS*
This bustling indoor/outdoor bazaar attracts vendors from across the country, selling exotic jewelry, rare records, and beautiful handmade furniture every weekend. Fresh seafood and gourmet treats are available daily.

MAP 3 E6 Ⓢ 32   225 7TH ST. SE
202-544-0083

FAIRY GODMOTHER   *KIDS STUFF*
Carrying equal amounts of fiction and nonfiction, Fairy Godmother lines its shelves with children's and young adult books hand-selected by the owner. Cool baby and creative arts toys give shoppers non-book options, too.

MAP 3 F6 Ⓢ 37   319 7TH ST. SE
202-547-5474

FLIGHTS OF FANCY   *KIDS STUFF*
Plush animals and marionettes comprise the decor, as well as the merchandise, of this well-stocked store. Also find an extensive collection of board games for both children and grown-ups.

MAP 3 B3 Ⓢ 5   UNION STATION, 50 MASSACHUSETTS AVE. NE
202-371-9800

THE FORECAST   *CLOTHING*
Helpful sales people will dress you up in luxurious, comfortable fabrics – silk, leather, suede, and velvet – from designers like Eileen Fisher, Yansi Fugel, and Michael Stars.

MAP 3 E6 Ⓢ 33   218 7TH ST. SE
202-547-7337

TROVER SHOP   *BOOKS*
A local bookstore that's been in D.C. since the 1960s, Trover carries bestsellers and a vast array of D.C. guidebooks and maps. Kids books and greeting cards let you shop for others, too.

MAP 3 E4 Ⓢ 23   221 PENNSYLVANIA AVE. SE
202-547-2665

THE VILLAGE   *CLOTHING*
An eclectic store with handcrafted items from around the world, The

ART & SOUL   EASTERN MARKET   APPALACHIAN SPRING

Village carries casual, comfortable clothing from Putumayo and Flax, in addition to various arts and crafts pieces.

MAP **3** E6 **S** 31   705 NORTH CAROLINA AVE. SE
202-546-3040

WOVEN HISTORY/SILK ROAD   *GIFT AND HOME*
One side of the store has woven rugs and tapestries from 30 locations in Asia, including Turkey and Nepal; the other carries antique furniture, textiles, and art from countries along the Silk Road.

MAP **3** F6 **S** 36   311-315 7TH ST. SE
202-543-1705

MAP **4** GEORGETOWN

APPALACHIAN SPRING   *GIFT AND HOME*
The perfect place for arty gifts and housewares, this decades-old store carries quality American crafts, including carved wooden boxes and kaleidoscopes, quilts, and hand-blown glass bowls and vases.

MAP **4** D4 **S** 11   1415 WISCONSIN AVE. NW
202-337-5780

BARNES & NOBLE BOOKSELLERS   *BOOKS AND MUSIC*
Browse the books, sample some CDs, or sip an espresso at this bustling three-level store. Look out for special events like book signings and author readings with the likes of Scott Turow.

MAP **4** E5 **S** 35   3040 M ST. NW
202-965-9880

BETSEY JOHNSON   *CLOTHING*
The offerings at this pink-walled boutique are gauzy, velvety, and always trendy. The look is hip, the clothes are small; waifs will do well here.

MAP **4** D4 **S** 12   1319 WISCONSIN AVE. NW
202-338-4090

BEYOND COMICS 2   *BOOKS*
Not just for comic store aficionados – though they'll find much to

love here, too — this store has books and action figures covering a wide variety of TV, movie, and animated heroes.

MAP 4 E5 **S34** 3060 M ST. NW
202-333-8651

DEAN & DELUCA *GOURMET GOODIES*
The gourmet store to end all gourmet stores, Dean & Deluca not only has superb groceries, but also beautiful knives, pans, and even sushi mats in the back.

MAP 4 E4 **S25** 3276 M ST. NW
202-342-2500

DEJA BLUE *CLOTHING*
The neon sign in the window reads, "thousands of old jeans," and that's just what you'll find at this specialty shop. No doubt there will be a pair perfect for you.

MAP 4 E5 **S32** 3005 M ST. NW
202-337-7100

DREAM DRESSER *CLOTHING*
Get your fetish fix here. A local legend, this racy shop overflows with leather and lace — scanty clothes, strappy accessories, and toys for behind closed doors.

MAP 4 F4 **S45** 1042 WISCONSIN AVE. NW
202-625-0373

FIRE AND ICE OF GEORGETOWN *JEWELRY*
Silver and semiprecious stones are the attention-grabbers, but glassware, numerous animal trinkets, and polished fossils are also on display at this special jewelry store.

MAP 4 E4 **S26** GEORGETOWN PARK MALL, 3222 M ST. NW
202-338-0024

FRANK MILWEE ANTIQUES *ANTIQUES*
Looking for an antique corkscrew? A pewter ice bucket? A cut-glass

cigar ashtray? This store carries the most vintage barware you'll ever see in one place.

MAP **4** E6 **$42** 2912 M ST. NW
202-333-4811

GEORGETOWN *SHOPPING DISTRICTS*
Stomping ground of the impossibly thin, impossibly tan, and impossibly rich, Georgetown combines capitalism with historic charm. Upscale boutiques stand near quaint rowhouses with cobblestone walkways, and mom-and-pop shops hold their own alongside mammoth chains.

MAP **4** E4 **$29** M ST. BTWN. 27TH AND 35TH STS. NW; WISCONSIN AVE.
BTWN. M AND S STS. NW

ILO DAY SPA *BATH, BEAUTY, AND SPA*
The European-trained specialists at this full-service teaching salon mean Saturday appointments go in a heartbeat, often to high-profile celebrities.

MAP **4** C4 **$8** 1637 WISCONSIN AVE. NW
202-342-0350

KEITH LIPERT GALLERY *ACCESSORIES*
A stunning collection of designer vases, candlesticks, scarves, handbags, and jewelry adorn the glass cabinets in this boutique. Mr. Lipert is usually there to show you around himself.

MAP **4** E6 **$39** 2922 M ST. NW
202-965-9736

MARSTON LUCE ANTIQUES *ANTIQUES*
Among the Provençal antiques offered here you'll find understated furniture and mirrors at affordable prices.

MAP **4** B3 **$3** 1651 WISCONSIN AVE. NW
202-333-6800

MICHAEL GETZ ANTIQUES *ANTIQUES*
The items in this random assortment have only Getz's taste in common. You'll find American, British, and continental antiques, with an interesting collection of andirons and other fireplace tools.

MAP **4** E6 **$41** 2918 M ST. NW
202-338-3811

MOVIE MADNESS *GIFT AND HOME*
An *Attack of the 50 Foot Woman* poster greets you at the entry of this movie lover's paradise. Inside are posters from all your favorite films.

MAP **4** E5 **$36** 1083 THOMAS JEFFERSON ST. NW
202-337-7064

ROCHE SALON *BATH, BEAUTY, AND SPA*
Considered one of the best cut and color shops in the city, this trendy salon is worth a visit just to see the wild and whimsical decor.

MAP **4** F5 **$50** 3050 K ST. NW
202-775-0775

MAP 5 DUPONT CIRCLE

BEADAZZLED *GIFT AND HOME*
Beadazzled has hundreds of containers, organized by color and filled with beads of every shape and size, from whimsical animals to semi-precious stones.

MAP 5 B5 ⑤ 25 1507 CONNECTICUT AVE. NW
202-265-2323

BETSY FISHER *CLOTHING*
Get personal attention while trying on individualistic clothes for working women from Diane von Furstenberg, Lacroix, and other midpriced designers. Play clothes and festive eveningwear round out the wardrobe selections.

MAP 5 C5 ⑤ 35 1224 CONNECTICUT AVE. NW
202-785-1975

BORDERS BOOKS AND MUSIC *BOOKS AND MUSIC*
In addition to the extensive book and music offerings, the full-scale cultural mix at Borders includes live jazz, wine tastings, film screenings, poetry slams, and author readings.

MAP 5 D5 ⑤ 52 1800 L ST. NW
202-466-4999

CHOCOLATE MOOSE *GIFT AND HOME*
This is a classy tchotchke store with amusing pins, hair accessories, candy, "bad girl" drink coasters, gag gifts, stickers, greeting cards, and games.

MAP 5 C5 ⑤ 49 1800 M ST. NW
202-463-0992

CHURCH'S ENGLISH SHOES *SHOES*
At this old-school men's shoe store, someone will sit at your feet and measure your foot size before offering you a choice from the selection of classic, conservative leather shoes. Stop in here for the right shoes to wear to a meeting on the Hill.

MAP 5 D5 ⑤ 51 1820 L ST. NW
202-296-3366

CLAUDE TAYLOR PHOTOGRAPHY *KIDS STUFF*
The merchandise theme here is characters from French children's books: Babar lunchboxes, Tintin books, Little Prince mugs. They also have a great collection of Parisian photos and posters.

MAP 5 A5 ⑤ 6 1627 CONNECTICUT AVE. NW
202-518-4000

COFFEE AND THE WORKS *GOURMET GOODIES*
There's barely room to move around in this overstuffed store, filled with coffee makers, teapots, and floor-to-ceiling bins of coffee beans, with gourmet cookware in the back.

MAP 5 A5 ⑤ 5 1627 CONNECTICUT AVE. NW
202-483-8050

EVERETT HALL DESIGNS   KRAMERBOOKS & AFTERWORDS

CUSTOM SHOP CLOTHIERS *CLOTHING*
Get measured, pick the fabric, and in 6-8 weeks you'll have a shirt
or suit tailored just for you. Styles are conservative, and prices
range from $89 shirts to $1,000 suits.

MAP 5 D6 ⑤57 1033 CONNECTICUT AVE. NW
202-659-8250

DUPONT CIRCLE *SHOPPING DISTRICTS*
Vibrant all day and especially at night when many businesses stay
open until 1 A.M., Dupont is Washington's pulse. The mix of chic boutiques, popular chains, and see-and-be-seen eateries – all of which
are gay friendly – ensure that you'll be well outfitted, well read, and
well fed.

MAP 5 B5 ⑤28 CONNECTICUT AVE. BTWN. K AND S STS. NW

EVERETT HALL DESIGNS *CLOTHING AND SHOES*
Celebrities and dignitaries shop here. Designer Everett Hall's fashionable suits can be bright and dramatic, but he'll also tailor something more somber just for you.

MAP 5 C5 ⑤34 1230 CONNECTICUT AVE. NW
202-467-0003

FRANZ BADER BOOKSTORE *BOOKS*
From coffee-table books to instructional manuals, art literature is
the focus here. Find books on graphic arts, fine arts, photography,
and architecture.

MAP 5 E5 ⑤62 1911 I ST. NW
202-337-5440

J & R CIGAR *GIFT AND HOME*
The floor-to-ceiling array of cigars here come from numerous countries – some as far-flung as Cameroon and Tanzania. Find handsome
wooden humidors and other cigar paraphernalia as well.

MAP 5 D6 ⑤56 1730 L ST. NW
202-296-3872

KRAMERBOOKS & AFTERWORDS *BOOKS*
This thriving independent bookstore shelves an excellent collection

TINY JEWEL BOX   ANDRE CHREKY

of new and local titles, along with an impressive cookbook and travel section. The café in the back provides a cozy spot to read.

MAP **5** B5 **S** 24   1517 CONNECTICUT AVE. NW
202-387-1400

LAMBDA RISING *BOOKS AND MUSIC*
The cheerful heart of Dupont's gay community, Lambda Rising was D.C.'s first bookstore for queer men and women when it was founded in 1974.

MAP **5** A5 **S** 7   1625 CONNECTICUT AVE. NW
202-462-6969

MELODY RECORDS *MUSIC*
The crammed aisles of rare finds and popular music at this no-frills storefront keep Dupont-area hipsters happy – even if the brooding folks behind the counter aren't.

MAP **5** A5 **S** 8   1623 CONNECTICUT AVE. NW
202-232-4002

PROPER TOPPER *ACCESSORIES*
Originally just a hat store, Propper Topper now goes beyond fedoras and glamorous cloches; scarves, gloves, jewelry, and wonderful bath soaps add even more elegance.

MAP **5** C5 **S** 31   1350 CONNECTICUT AVE. NW
202-842-3055

RIZIK BROTHERS *CLOTHING*
Since 1908, Rizik's has supplied perfect (and pricey) outfits for crucial occasions – evening dresses, power suits, and wedding gowns – from both contemporary and classic designers.

MAP **5** D6 **S** 55   1100 CONNECTICUT AVE. NW
202-223-4050

SALON DANIEL *BATH, BEAUTY, AND SPA*
Young professionals, male and female, frequent this busy salon, which occupies a three-story townhouse. Hair, nail, and skin treatments are available, usually on the day you call.

MAP **5** C5 **S** 36   1831 M ST. NW
202-296-4856

SECOND STORY BOOKS & ANTIQUES   *BOOKS AND MUSIC*
A knowledgeable staff and an amazing collection of obscure, well-loved treasures (everything from old Hollywood to French lit) keep bookworms happy at this tiny, off-the-beaten-path hideaway.

MAP **5** B4 **S** 22   2000 P ST. NW
202-659-8884

TINY JEWEL BOX   *JEWELRY*
The owners of this D.C. institution search estate sales and work with designers to find one-of-a-kind pieces. Downstairs, ogle the expensive precious jewelry; upstairs, browse the modern, semiprecious, and faux pieces.

MAP **5** D6 **S** 53   1147 CONNECTICUT AVE. NW
202-393-2747

TOAST AND STRAWBERRIES   *CLOTHING*
Nothing here is mass-produced. Out-of-the-ordinary, bright clothing and decorative caftans are staples at this Dupont Circle boutique – one of the city's oldest black-owned stores.

MAP **5** A5 **S** 9   1608 CONNECTICUT AVE. NW
202-234-1212

THE WRITTEN WORD   *GIFT AND HOME*
Paper lovers will love the handmade sheets and artistic greeting cards here. Fancy pens, luxurious ribbons, and custom letterpressed personal stationery are available, too.

MAP **5** B5 **S** 29   1365 CONNECTICUT AVE. NW
202-223-1400

MAP **6** | LOGAN CIRCLE/U STREET

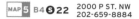

ADC MAP AND TRAVEL CENTER   *BOOKS AND MUSIC*
Cartography galore is crammed into this tiny storefront. Plot your escape with detailed maps, globes, and *National Geographic* paraphernalia.

MAP **6** F2 **S** 36   1636 I ST. NW
800-544-2659

ANDRE CHREKY   *BATH, BEAUTY, AND SPA*
Chic Washingtonians swear by this buzzed-about salon for the latest in cutting-edge hair design and trustworthy color. The decadent roster of seasonal spa services (fruit enzyme facials, for example) are a necessary indulgence.

MAP **6** F2 **S** 37   1604 K ST. NW
202-293-9393

CANDIDA'S WORLD OF BOOKS   *BOOKS AND MUSIC*
This down-to-earth haven for bookworms specializes in writings from and about other cultures. Travel guides are also a plentiful here.

MAP **6** C3 **S** 22   1541 14TH ST. NW
202-667-4811 OR 866-667-4811

NANA   FRIENDSHIP FLOWER SHOP

DA HSIN TRADING COMPANY   *GIFT AND HOME*

Spot the shop by the huge Chinese vases in the window. Inside find a motley stock, including ceramic bowls of all sizes, inexpensive chopsticks, parasols, and beaded curtains.

MAP 6 A2 **S** 46   811 7TH ST. NW
202-789-4020

NANA   *CLOTHING AND SHOES*

Nana deals new and used, vintage and brand-name duds, along with one-of-a-kind handbags and bath products, too. Members Only jackets, Hobo bags, and Preloved constructions are all in the mix here.

MAP 6 A2 **S** 2   1534 U ST. NW
202-667-6955

POP   *CLOTHING*

Wacky apparel and modish accessories — such as fluorescent Penguin shirts, retro Ben Sherman jeans, and limited edition watches and jewelry — fly off the shelves at this candy-colored monument to pop culture goodies.

MAP 6 B3 **S** 15   1803-A 14TH ST. NW
202-332-3312

PULP   *GIFT AND HOME*

This stationery store makes a statement. Unique writing materials, mod cards, and other hipster accoutrements lure an edgy crowd.

MAP 6 B3 **S** 14   1805 ½ 14TH ST. NW
202-462-7857

U STREET   *SHOPPING DISTRICTS*

The epicenter of chic in D.C., "New U" is fast becoming a gentrified haven for vintage clothing shops (Nana, Wild Women Wear Red), urban furniture fixtures (Habitat, Home Rule), and sleek boutiques (Maison 14, Pop).

MAP 6 A1 **S** 1   U ST. BTWN. 12TH AND 18TH STS. NW

MAP 7 UPPER NORTHWEST

ARTISAN LAMP COMPANY *GIFT AND HOME*
Except for some small art nouveau lamps, the antiques here are siz-able. The selection includes heavy floor lamps, glittering chandeliers, and rococo mirrors. Many are expensive; everything is out of the ordinary.

MAP 7 A6 ❺ 9 3331 CONNECTICUT AVE. NW
202-244-8900

FRIENDSHIP FLOWER SHOP *GIFT AND HOME*
This family-run horticultural heaven has been in bloom for more than 50 years. Exotic Hawaiian blossoms, seasonal arrangements, and lovely plants flourish here.

MAP 7 B2 ❺ 15 3226 WISCONSIN AVE. NW
202-966-4405

SULLIVAN'S TOY STORE *KIDS STUFF*
Stocking both handmade and more mainstream toys, this cozy, family-owned spot is a great place to let kids' imaginations run wild.

MAP 7 A2 ❺ 1 3412 WISCONSIN AVE. NW
202-362-1343

VACE *GOURMET GOODIES*
Vace's succulent specialties are perfect for an Italian feast. After stocking up on authentic groceries, such as homemade pizza dough and imported prosciutto, grab a crisp slice of pizza from the to-go counter.

MAP 7 B6 ❺ 18 3315 CONNECTICUT AVE. NW
202-363-1999

WAKE UP LITTLE SUZIE *GIFT AND HOME*
Pottery, jewelry, and glasswork fill this small Cleveland Park store. Objects range from small knickknacks and greeting cards to more expensive art pieces.

MAP 7 A6 ❺ 7 3409 CONNECTICUT AVE. NW
202-244-0700

MAP 8 ADAMS MORGAN

ALL ABOUT JANE *CLOTHING*
The inventory is small, but it packs a punch. The casual clothes are fun and stylish: Juicy Couture denim, flowery Laundry tanks, and Shoshanna bikinis.

MAP 8 D5 ❺ 24 2438 ½ 18TH ST. NW
202-797-9710

ALL WRAPPED UP *GIFT AND HOME*
Cards, wrapping paper, candles, books, and unique gifts fill this

BRASS KNOB ARCHITECTURAL ANTIQUES

SHAKE YOUR BOOTY

sweet store. The merchandise is always in theme with the season, so look here first for Valentine's Day and Halloween accessories.

MAP 8 B3 S 2   2643 CONNECTICUT AVE. NW
202-332-2222

ANTIQUES ANONYMOUS   *VINTAGE AND ANTIQUES*
Boxy purses and gauzy vintage dresses pack the racks in this small store, but the real find is the jewelry. These cameos and antique styles can't be found elsewhere.

MAP 8 C3 S 6   2627 CONNECTICUT AVE. NW
202-332-5555

BLUE MERCURY   *BATH, BEAUTY, AND SPA*
Carrying the most select (and expensive) facial products and make-up, Blue Mercury is a small chain that stocks magazine-referenced brands like Bliss, Creed, and Trish McEvoy.

MAP 8 F4 S 49   1745 CONNECTICUT AVE. NW
202-462-1300

BOMBE CHEST   *ANTIQUES*
This cluttered consignment store benefits the Jewish Social Service Agency. Find sterling silver place settings, glass decanters, candlesticks, vases, paintings, and some Judaica.

MAP 8 C3 S 5   2629 CONNECTICUT AVE. NW
202-387-7293

BRASS KNOB ARCHITECTURAL ANTIQUES
ANTIQUES
In addition to the many antique doorknobs, this shop also carries numerous antique light fixtures, stone accents, and other decorative hardware.

MAP 8 D5 S 31   2311 18TH ST. NW
202-332-3370

DAISY   *CLOTHING AND SHOES*
Girly, colorful clothes fill this California-style boutique. Designers like Diane von Furstenberg, Billy Blues, and Hollywould provide Daisy's pastel tees, cool sunglasses, high heels, and jeans in every style.

MAP 8 C5 S 9   1814 ADAMS MILL RD. NW
202-797-1777

18TH STREET *SHOPPING DISTRICTS*
With shops and restaurants of every ethnic persuasion, this well-worn strip is the lifeblood of Adams Morgan. Culture vultures share sidewalk space with fortune tellers and street vendors as they peruse the edgy offerings.

MAP 8 E5 ⑤39   18 ST. NW BTWN. SWANN AND CALVERT STS. NW

GINZA *GIFT AND HOME*
Traditional Japanese teacups, sake carafes, and chopstick sets rest on wooden shelves in this Asian-themed store. They have a small collection of Japanese art and language books, too.

MAP 8 F4 ⑤50   1721 CONNECTICUT AVE. NW
202-331-7991

IDLE TIME BOOKS *BOOKS AND MUSIC*
Idle Time is an earthy source for inexpensive, used books on every topic from Malaysian cooking to feminist literary criticism.

MAP 8 C5 ⑤14   2467 18TH ST. NW
202-232-4774

SHAKE YOUR BOOTY *CLOTHING AND SHOES*
Come here for the latest in shoes and purses, in bright colors and this season's styles. Seek out the sale table for that great, cut-price find.

MAP 8 D5 ⑤29   2324 18TH ST. NW
202-518-8205

SKYNEAR AND CO. *GIFT AND HOME*
A five-foot, baby blue Egyptian cat perches outside the window of this eclectic store. Inside find unique furniture, ultramodern lamps, and kitschy purses.

MAP 8 D5 ⑤33   2122 18TH ST. NW
202-797-7160

OVERVIEW MAP AND OFF MAP

POLITICS & PROSE BOOKSTORE AND COFFEEHOUSE
BOOKS AND MUSIC
This intimate bookstore is a favorite for the Washington cognoscenti, who enjoy sipping espresso while browsing the great selection of political must-reads. High-profile events – Bill Clinton, Molly Ivins, Gary Hart – are also a plus.

OFF MAP   5015 CONNECTICUT AVE. NW
202-364-1919

REPRINT BOOKSHOP *BOOKS*
This thriving indie bookstore brings a touch of culture to a staid government neighborhood. Many big-name authors, including Anita Hill, have stopped here to chat about their work.

OVERVIEW MAP E4   456 L'ENFANT PLZ. SW
202-554-5070

ARTS AND LEISURE

Best small gallery: **ZENITH GALLERY,** p. 72

Best local art: **SPECTRUM GALLERY,** p. 73

Best American art: **CORCORAN MUSEUM OF ART,** p. 68

Best museum gardens: **DUMBARTON OAKS,** p. 72

Best museum shop: **NATIONAL BUILDING MUSEUM,** p. 70

Best place to see a blockbuster:
LOEWS CINEPLEX ODEON UPTOWN, p. 81

The place to see the latest art flick:
VISIONS CINEMA BISTRO LOUNGE, p. 81

Common ground for history and theater buffs:
FORD'S THEATRE, p. 78

Best concert ambience: **DUMBARTON CHURCH CONCERTS,** p. 80

D.C.'s destination performing arts complex: **JOHN F. KENNEDY CENTER FOR THE PERFORMING ARTS,** p. 76

Best spot to recharge from museum fatigue:
NATIONAL GALLERY OF ART SCULPTURE GARDEN, p. 84

Best in-city escape from the city: **ROCK CREEK PARK,** p. 87

Best place to travel back in time:
CHESAPEAKE & OHIO CANAL NATIONAL HISTORIC PARK, p. 85

Best views of cherry blossoms:
along the Tidal Basin in **WEST POTOMAC PARK,** p. 83

Best urban people-watching: **DUPONT CIRCLE,** p. 86

MUSEUMS AND GALLERIES

MAP 1 | WESTERN MALL/FOGGY BOTTOM

ART MUSEUM OF THE AMERICAS
The changing exhibitions here emphasize the art and culture of Latin America and the Caribbean. The museum's ornate Spanish colonial home features exterior iron grillwork and richly colored tiles.

MAP 1 C4 35   201 18TH ST. NW
202-458-6016

CORCORAN MUSEUM OF ART
Among the treasures found in D.C.'s largest privately funded institution are Gilbert Stuart's famous portrait of George Washington and Frederic Church's stunning landscape, *Niagara*.

MAP 1 B5 30   500 17TH ST. NW
202-639-1700

DAUGHTERS OF THE AMERICAN REVOLUTION MUSEUM
Collecting quilts, plates, and other ephemera from the Revolution through the early 1900s, the D.A.R. Museum centers around historical reproductions of interior spaces. Among the 31 period rooms are a colonial parlor, a tavern, and a church.

MAP 1 C5 36   1776 D ST. NW
202-879-3241

DECATUR HOUSE
Designed by America's first professional architect, Benjamin Henry Latrobe, this 1818 brick residence accommodated international dignitaries for more than a century. Museum collections include fine and decorative art from the period.

MAP 1 A5 9   748 JACKSON PL. NW
202-842-0920

EISENHOWER EXECUTIVE OFFICE BUILDING
Take a tour of this multitiered wedding cake of a building, finished 1888 and restored nearly a century later. This was once the home of the Departments of State, War, and Navy.

MAP 1 B5 28   17TH ST. AND PENNSYLVANIA AVE. NW
202-395-5895

THE OCTAGON MUSEUM
Once home to President Madison after the White House burned down in 1814, the Octagon hosts architectural and decorative art

CORCORAN MUSEUM OF ART   ARTHUR M. SACKLER GALLERY

exhibits in its meticulously restored Federal-style – though not eight-sided – building.

MAP 1 B4 ⓐ 26   1799 NEW YORK AVE. NW
202-638-3221

RENWICK GALLERY
This Smithsonian museum displays the best in American crafts, paintings, and decorative arts of today and yesterday in an ornate Second Empire-style building. Don't miss the stunning handcrafted furniture on the first floor.

MAP 1 A5 ⓐ 14   17TH ST. AND PENNSYLVANIA AVE. NW
202-633-2850

UNITED STATES DEPARTMENT OF THE INTERIOR MUSEUM
Exhibits highlight our government's role in Native American affairs, wildlife management, and geologic research. Afterwards, walk around to admire the grand 1930s-era Interior Building with its 25 murals and sculptures.

MAP 1 C4 ⓐ 33   1849 C ST. NW
202-208-4743

MAP 2 | CENTRAL MALL/SMITHSONIAN

ARTHUR M. SACKLER GALLERY
The Sackler's Asian treasures include fine objects decorated with Chinese jade and an extensive collection of Islamic manuscripts. For more works from the Far East, the gallery links underground to the Freer Gallery of Art.

MAP 2 E3 ⓐ 59   1050 INDEPENDENCE AVE. SW
202-633-4880

EKLEKTIKOS GALLERY OF CONTEMPORARY ART
The name is Greek for "eclectic," which describes the range of this architecturally dramatic gallery showing contemporary work by regional and international artists.

MAP 2 C4 ⓐ 45   406 7TH ST. NW, 3RD FL.
202-783-8444

HIRSHHORN MUSEUM AND
SCULPTURE GARDEN

INTERNATIONAL SPY MUSEUM

FREER GALLERY OF ART
Displaying masterpieces in a beautiful Italian Renaissance-style
building, this Smithsonian museum, along with the Sackler Gallery,
makes up the national museum of Asian art.

MAP 2 E3 ⓐ58   INDEPENDENCE AVE. AND 12TH ST. SW
202-633-4880

HIRSHHORN MUSEUM AND SCULPTURE GARDEN
Go to the Hirshhorn, the Smithsonian's modern art space, for
impressive works by Henry Moore, Picasso, and Rodin, but especially
for art created in the last 25 years.

MAP 2 E4 ⓐ61   7TH ST. AND INDEPENDENCE AVE., SW
202-633-4674

INTERNATIONAL SPY MUSEUM
Interactive multimedia presentations, photography, and artifacts
provide a historical examination of espionage around the world.
Highlights include a collection of eye-popping spy gadgetry and film
interviews with former CIA and KGB agents.

MAP 2 B4 ⓐ29   800 F ST. NW
202-393-7798

NATIONAL AIR AND SPACE MUSEUM
See SIGHTS, p. 8.

MAP 2 E5 ✪62   INDEPENDENCE AVE. AND 4TH ST. SW
202-357-2700

NATIONAL AQUARIUM
The nation's oldest aquarium is inside the Department of Commerce.
Feed the piranhas, scare the sharks, or see any of the other 1,200
species on display.

MAP 2 C1 ⓐ39   14TH ST. AND CONSTITUTION AVE. NW
202-482-2826

NATIONAL ARCHIVES
See SIGHTS, p. 8.

MAP 2 C4 ✪49   CONSTITUTION AVE. BTWN. 7TH AND 9TH STS. NW
866-272-6272

NATIONAL BUILDING MUSEUM
Stretching more than 300 feet in length and incorporating eight

gigantic Corinthian columns, the museum's Great Hall is the main attraction here, but don't miss the thought-provoking exhibits on modern architecture.

MAP **2** B6 **38**   401 F ST. NW
202-272-2448

NATIONAL GALLERY OF ART

See SIGHTS, p. 9.

MAP **2** D5 **54**   4TH ST. AND CONSTITUTION AVE. NW
202-737-4215

NATIONAL MUSEUM OF AFRICAN ART

Located underground in the Smithsonian Quadrangle complex, the museum's permanent collection of more than 7,000 items will enhance your understanding of hundreds of African cultures.

MAP **2** E3 **60**   950 INDEPENDENCE AVE. SW
202-633-4600

NATIONAL MUSEUM OF AMERICAN HISTORY

Three floors of artifacts chronicle America's rich history. Included are the original Star-Spangled Banner, a Model-T Ford, and Dorothy's ruby slippers.

MAP **2** D2 **51**   14TH ST. AND CONSTITUTION AVE. NW
202-357-2700

NATIONAL MUSEUM OF NATURAL HISTORY

The nation's largest research museum is stuffed with more than 121 million specimens of fossils, plants, animals, and gems. The Hope Diamond is on permanent display.

MAP **2** D3 **52**   10TH ST. AND CONSTITUTION AVE. NW
202-357-2700

NATIONAL MUSEUM OF THE AMERICAN INDIAN

Opened in September 2004, this third branch of the NMAI highlights Native American culture and achievement. Permanent exhibits focus on worldviews, peoples, and contemporary issues, and theme- or artist-based shows comprise the temporary offerings.

MAP **2** E6 **63**   4TH ST. AND INDEPENDENCE AVE. SW
202-633-1000

NAVAL HERITAGE CENTER

Come search the computers for records of your favorite Navy veteran. Afterward, an exciting short film, *At Sea,* will put you aboard a modern aircraft carrier.

MAP **2** C4 **48**   701 PENNSYLVANIA AVE. NW
202-737-2300 OR 800-821-8892

SMITHSONIAN INSTITUTION

See SIGHTS, p. 10.

MAP **2** E3 **57**   1000 JEFFERSON DR. NW
202-633-1000

UNITED STATES HOLOCAUST MEMORIAL MUSEUM

See SIGHTS, p. 11.

MAP **2** E2 **64**   100 RAOUL WALLENBERG PL. SW
202-488-0400, 800-400-9373 (TIMED ENTRY PASSES FOR EXHIBITION HALL)

DUMBARTON OAKS   THE OLD STONE HOUSE

ZENITH GALLERY
Founded in 1978, Zenith is one of the most eclectic private galleries in Washington, offering a well-known collection of contemporary art that includes sculptures, ceramics, glass, and neon art.

MAP **2** B4 **Ⓐ36**   413 7TH ST. NW
202-783-2963

MAP 3 | CAPITOL HILL

FOLGER SHAKESPEARE LIBRARY
Besides hosting chamber music concerts, exhibits, lectures, and theatrical productions, this award-winning art deco building is filled with the world's largest collection of works by and about the Bard.

MAP **3** E4 **Ⓐ22**   201 E. CAPITOL ST. SE
202-544-4600

NATIONAL POSTAL MUSEUM
An enormous collection of stamps and three vintage mail planes are among the interesting exhibits that put a unique spin on U.S. postal history.

MAP **3** B2 **Ⓐ1**   2 MASSACHUSETTS AVE. NE
202-633-8181

MAP 4 | GEORGETOWN

ADDISON/RIPLEY FINE ART
Amid the antique shops and cafés of fashionable upper Georgetown, this spacious gallery offers a mix of contemporary, regional, and international painting and photography.

MAP **4** B3 **Ⓐ2**   1670 WISCONSIN AVE. NW
202-338-5180

DUMBARTON OAKS
Harvard University maintains the excellent collection of paintings, rare books, Byzantine coins, and pre-Columbian artifacts in this

expansive 19th-century home. Outside, 10 acres of gardens are a treat year-round.

`MAP 4` B4 Ⓐ5   1703 32ND ST. NW
202-339-6400

FINE ART & ARTISTS
This three-story rowhouse is devoted to pop and contemporary masters, including Lichtenstein, Warhol, and Rauschenberg. A courtyard garden features rotating exhibits by contemporary artists.

`MAP 4` E6 Ⓐ40   2920 M ST. NW
202-965-0780

FRASER GALLERY
The emphasis of the Fraser Gallery, considered a showplace for the stars of the local arts scene, is on contemporary realism and black-and-white photography.

`MAP 4` F5 Ⓐ47   1054 31ST ST. NW
202-298-6450

GOVINDA GALLERY
Annie Leibovitz had her first D.C. show here in 1984, kicking off the gallery's well-earned reputation as a mainstay for rock-and-roll photography.

`MAP 4` E3 Ⓐ16   1227 34TH ST. NW
202-333-1180

THE OLD STONE HOUSE
Tucked into Georgetown's busiest shopping street, this original 18th-century home is a window into simpler times. The large backyard garden is a breathtaking surprise.

`MAP 4` E5 Ⓐ31   3051 M ST. NW
202-426-6851

SPECTRUM GALLERY
The original offerings at Georgetown's oldest gallery (owned and managed by thirty local artists) include landscapes, photography, prints, and sculpture. Punctuating the collection is an exhibit by the local artist of the month.

`MAP 4` F6 Ⓐ52   1132 29TH ST. NW
202-333-0954

MAP 5 | DUPONT CIRCLE

ALEX GALLERY
Filling three full floors of space, this is one of the largest galleries in Dupont Circle and features contemporary paintings and sculptures by American and European artists.

`MAP 5` A4 Ⓐ1   2106 R ST. NW
202-667-2599

KATHLEEN EWING GALLERY
Almost a D.C. institution, this gallery shows vintage and contemporary photography in a friendly apartmentlike atmosphere.

MAP 5 A5 ● 10   1609 CONNECTICUT AVE. NW
202-328-0955

MARSHA MATEYKA GALLERY
This perfectly preserved late-19th century townhouse creates an intimate setting for colorful contemporary paintings and drawings. Guggenheim Fellow Gene Davis is among the well-established artists represented here.

MAP 5 A4 ● 2   2012 R ST. NW
202-328-0088

THE PHILLIPS COLLECTION
Started as just two rooms in the Phillips family's personal residence, the nation's first modern art museum is also one of Washington's most beautiful spaces. Diebenkorns, Mondrians, Rothkos, and the like comprise this fine collection.

MAP 5 A4 ● 4   1600 21ST ST. NW
202-387-2151

THE SOCIETY OF THE CINCINNATI
The Society was established in 1783 by George Washington and his officers. The beaux arts mansion contains a large collection of European and Asian fine arts and antiques, as well as artifacts from the American Revolution.

MAP 5 B4 ● 14   2118 MASSACHUSETTS AVE. NW
202-785-2040

MAP 6 | LOGAN CIRCLE/U STREET

MARY MCLEOD BETHUNE COUNCIL HOUSE
Formerly the headquarters of the National Council of Negro Women, this restored 19th-century townhouse now houses a museum and the National Archives for Black Women's History.

MAP 6 D4 ● 29   1318 VERMONT AVE. NW
202-673-2402

THE NATIONAL GEOGRAPHIC MUSEUM AT EXPLORERS HALL
Interactive displays put the Society's wealth of knowledge at your fingertips, and a small gallery showcases a new world-class photography exhibit every month.

MAP 6 E2 ● 31   1145 17TH ST. NW
202-857-7588

NATIONAL MUSEUM OF WOMEN IN THE ARTS
At the only museum exclusively carrying the works of women artists, the mixed-media collections include lesser-knowns as well as superstars like Georgia O'Keeffe, Mary Cassatt, and Frida Kahlo.

MAP 6 F4 ● 44   1250 NEW YORK AVE. NW
202-783-5000 OR 800-222-7270

MAP 8 | ADAMS MORGAN

CONNER CONTEMPORARY ART
Whether it's abstract sculpture, colorful pop art, contemporary photography, or digital media, the work shown in this small gallery's monthly exhibits is always some of the most original in Washington.

MAP 8 F4 ⬤ 46 1730 CONNECTICUT AVE. NW, 2ND FL.
202-588-8750

DISTRICT OF COLUMBIA ARTS CENTER
A cornerstone of the Washington arts scene, DCAC exhibits local artists' works, including metallic sculptures, mixed-media paintings, and video performance art. The black box theater has films, plays, and improv comedy.

MAP 8 D5 ⬤ 23 2438 18TH ST. NW
202-462-7833

IRVINE CONTEMPORARY ART
Striking a good balance between popular (colorful drawings) and more avant-garde (TV screens flashing hypnotic linear designs) material, this gallery appeals to a wide range of contemporary art fans.

MAP 8 F4 ⬤ 47 1710 CONNECTICUT AVE. NW
202-332-8767

THE TEXTILE MUSEUM
Inside the museum's two elegant townhouses are pre-Columbian, Egyptian, and Islamic textiles and a fine collection of Peruvian weavings. Outside, there's a lovely garden.

MAP 8 F3 ⬤ 44 2320 S ST. NW
202-667-0441

WOODROW WILSON HOUSE
Our 28th president chose this elegant brick townhouse for his retirement after leaving the White House. On display are trophies and souvenirs of his presidency.

MAP 8 F3 ⬤ 43 2340 S ST. NW
202-387-4062

PERFORMING ARTS

MAP 1 | WESTERN MALL/FOGGY BOTTOM

AMERICAN FILM INSTITUTE NATIONAL FILM THEATER
MOVIE HOUSE

This gem of a theater serves up cinema for the intellectual set. Classics and obscurities alike show up on the calendar, along with mini-film fests by genre or artist.

MAP 1 B1◊25   KENNEDY CENTER, 2700 F ST. NW
202-833-2348

DAR CONSTITUTION HALL *MUSIC*

Every president since Calvin Coolidge has attended an event at Constitution Hall. A variety of superstars, from pop music's Bruce Springsteen to opera's Cecilia Bartoli, find their way to the stage of this giant neoclassical venue.

MAP 1 C4◊34   311 18TH ST. NW
202-628-4780

DOROTHY BETTS MARVIN THEATER *VARIOUS*

Located on campus in the Marvin Center, this theater stages professional performances by George Washington University's theater, music, and dance departments year-round.

MAP 1 A3◊4   MARVIN CENTER, 800 21ST ST. NW
202-994-6178

EISENHOWER THEATER *VARIOUS*

The 1,100-seat Eisenhower brings in surprises and star power with its array of contemporary dance, ballet, theatrical productions, and musicals.

MAP 1 B1◊19   KENNEDY CENTER, 2700 F ST. NW
202-467-4600 OR 202-416-8000

JOHN F. KENNEDY CENTER FOR THE PERFORMING ARTS
VARIOUS

Ever since it opened in the early '70s, the Kennedy Center has anchored the performing arts scene in D.C. The center's five theaters present an ever-changing mix of offerings, including opera, music festivals, plays, dance, and musicals.

MAP 1 B1◊18   2700 F ST. NW
202-416-8340

KENNEDY CENTER OPERA HOUSE *OPERA*

The Washington National Opera, under the artistic direction of Placido Domingo, mounts beautiful productions in this 2,200-seat

JOHN F. KENNEDY CENTER FOR
THE PERFORMING ARTS

KENNEDY CENTER OPERA HOUSE

house. It is also the opulent setting for dance extravaganzas and large-scale musicals.

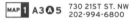 **MAP 1** B1 **20** KENNEDY CENTER, 2700 F ST. NW
202-295-2400 OR 202-416-8000

LISNER AUDITORIUM *MUSIC*
The eclectic roster at this George Washington University theater runs the gamut from jazz great Quincy Jones to Engelbert Humperdinck to Buddhist musical festivals.

MAP 1 A3 **5** 730 21ST ST. NW
202-994-6800

MILLENNIUM STAGE *MUSIC*
This stage in the Kennedy Center's Grand Foyer brings art to the masses with free performances (mainly musical, with occasional comedy, dance, and readings) daily at 6 P.M. No tickets are required, just show up – the earlier the better.

MAP 1 B1 **21** KENNEDY CENTER, 2700 F ST. NW
202-467-4600 OR 202-416-8000

NATIONAL SYMPHONY ORCHESTRA *MUSIC*
This renowned orchestra mounts a seemingly infinite variety of programs include visiting conductors, pianists, violinists, and vocalists.

MAP 1 B1 **24** KENNEDY CENTER CONCERT HALL, 2700 F ST. NW
202-467-4600 OR 202-416-8000

SYLVAN THEATER *MUSIC*
This outdoor theater on the Washington Monument grounds comes alive in the summer with concerts by military bands and the National Symphony Orchestra.

MAP 1 D6 **43** NATIONAL MALL AT 15TH ST. AND INDEPENDENCE AVE. NW
202-619-7222

TERRACE THEATER *THEATER*
Philip Johnson-designed Terrace Theater presents chamber recitals and dramatic and experimental plays in its small, 513-seat space.

MAP 1 B1 **22** KENNEDY CENTER, 2700 F ST. NW
202-295-2400 OR 202-416-8000

THE GREAT OUTDOORS

There's just something about enjoying an outdoor performance on a warm summer evening – perhaps it's the romance or perhaps it's the relaxation. Either way, D.C. gives you plenty of options. On Monday nights in July and August, "Screen on the Green" (877-262-5866) shows classic films at sunset, under the shadow of the Washington Monument. Or, at the opposite end of the week, the **National Gallery's Sculpture Garden (p. 84)** hosts "Jazz in the Garden" every Friday night, 5–8 P.M., from early June to the beginning of September. Off the Mall, Rock Creek Park's Carter Barron Amphitheatre (16th St. and Colorado Ave. NW; 202-426-0486) kicks off their summer season with a week-long run of the **Shakespeare Theatre's (p. 79)** "Free for All." Bring a picnic to make the experience complete.

THEATER LAB *THEATER*
Known as the home of *Shear Madness,* an audience-participation suspense comedy about a murder in a beauty salon, the Theater Lab focuses primarily on programs for young people.

MAP 1 B1 ⓐ 23   KENNEDY CENTER, 2700 F ST. NW
202-467-4600 OR 202-416-8000

MAP 2 CENTRAL MALL/SMITHSONIAN

CAPITOL STEPS *COMEDY*
This troupe of current and former congressional staffers puts its own spin on the political world with hilarious spoofs and satirical songs every Friday and Saturday night.

MAP 2 B2 ⓐ 19   RONALD REAGAN BUILDING AND INTERNATIONAL TRADE
CENTER AMPHITHEATER, 1300 PENNSYLVANIA AVE. NW
202-312-1555

FORD'S THEATRE *THEATER*
History buffs flock to see where Abe Lincoln sat the night he was assassinated. Despite its violent past, Ford's productions are strictly family fare.

MAP 2 B3 ⓐ 26   511 10TH ST. NW
202-638-2941 OR 202-347-4833

LANDMARK'S E STREET CINEMA *MOVIE HOUSE*
Munch on a locally made pastry and sip an espresso while watching the latest independent, foreign, and documentary films. This eight-

screen indy movie house boasts stadium seating in seven of its theaters and Dolby Digital sound.

MAP 2 B3 ⊕24 555 11TH ST. NW
202-452-7672

MCI CENTER *MUSIC*
The home of D.C.'s own basketball and hockey teams, this 20,000-
seat downtown arena is where the likes of Madonna and Eric Clapton
sing when they come to town.

MAP 2 A5 ⊕8 601 F ST. NW
202-628-3200

NATIONAL THEATRE *THEATER*
Washington's take on the Great White Way, this 1835 landmark
mounts full-scale Broadway hits. Call for a schedule of free shows
and occasional films.

MAP 2 B2 ⊕17 1321 PENNSYLVANIA AVE. NW
202-628-6161

THE SHAKESPEARE THEATRE *THEATER*
This intimate 451-seat venue is counted among the finest performance spaces in the city. Under Michael Kahn's direction, the
theatre presents internationally acclaimed productions of works by
Shakespeare and other classic playwrights.

MAP 2 B4 ⊕34 450 7TH ST. NW
202-547-1122

WARNER THEATRE *VARIOUS*
Enjoy comedy, drama, jazz, or even a circus in the restored elegance
of this former 1920s movie house. The lobby bar opens one hour
before show time.

MAP 2 B2 ⊕18 513 13TH ST. NW
202-783-4000

MAP 3 CAPITOL HILL

AMC UNION STATION 9 *MOVIE HOUSE*
Its location inside Union Station's old storage catacombs gives this
otherwise typical nine-theater multiplex character. Just blocks from
the Capitol, this AMC is convenient to shopping, dining, and train
travel.

MAP 3 B3 ⊕6 UNION STATION, 50 MASSACHUSETTS AVE. NE
703-998-4262 OR 202-842-3757

COOLIDGE AUDITORIUM *MUSIC*
The excellent acoustics in this intimate Library of Congress hall
enhance the considerable talents of the visiting chamber groups,
string quartets, and, occasionally, soloists from the National
Symphony Orchestra.

MAP 3 E4 ⊕21 101 INDEPENDENCE AVE. SE
202-707-5000

SOURCE THEATRE COMPANY   LOEWS CINEPLEX ODEON UPTOWN

MAP 4 GEORGETOWN

DUMBARTON CHURCH CONCERTS *MUSIC*
Washington's best chamber music – classical, jazz, and early
music – is presented in historic Dumbarton Church October–May.
Concerts are candlelit for added ambience.

MAP 4 D5 **A**13   3133 DUMBARTON ST. NW
202-965-2000

MAP 6 LOGAN CIRCLE/U STREET

GALA HISPANIC THEATRE *THEATER*
The ongoing fare consists of bilingual productions, many with trans-
lation via headphones, of contemporary Spanish, Latin American,
and Latino plays. Check the schedule for frequent special events.

MAP 6 E6 **A**35   WAREHOUSE THEATER, 1021 7TH ST. NW
202-234-7174

HR-57 CENTER FOR PRESERVATION OF JAZZ AND BLUES
MUSIC
By day, this neighborhood cultural center hosts workshops and
classes on jazz and blues. At night, some of the area's best musicians illustrate how it's done. You can BYOB for a small corking fee.

MAP 6 C3 **A**21   1610 14TH ST. NW
202-667-3700

LINCOLN THEATRE *VARIOUS*
Lincoln Theatre recalls the heyday of the historic U Street district.
From circuses to gospel performances, this magnificently restored
1920s theater venue features a diverse spectrum of entertainment.

MAP 6 A4 **A**6   1215 U ST. NW
202-328-6000

SOURCE THEATRE COMPANY *THEATER*
This cutting edge, black box theater showcases modern plays and

revamped classics, tending toward the experimental. Spare bleacher seats keep your attention directed at the performers.

 **MAP 6** B3 **A** 12 1835 14TH ST. NW
202-462-1073

STANISLAVSKY THEATER STUDIO *THEATER*

STS performs adaptations of classic literature, incorporating dance, music, movement, and pantomime in a converted mid-19th-century brick building.

MAP 6 C1 **A** 16 1742 CHURCH ST. NW
202-265-3767

STUDIO THEATRE *THEATER*

There's not a bad seat in the house at this intimate theater-in-the-round – formerly an automobile repair shop. Studio's eclectic, contemporary offerings never disappoint, and the lobby café has great intermission treats.

MAP 6 C3 **A** 23 1333 P ST. NW
202-332-3300

THEATER J/AARON AND
CECILE GOLDMAN THEATER *VARIOUS*

Theater J performs an American-Jewish repertoire in the elegant 236-seat Aaron and Cecile Goldman Theater. The multifaceted space frequently plays host to music and film festivals, too.

MAP 6 C2 **A** 18 1529 16TH ST. NW
202-777-3229

MAP 7 | UPPER NORTHWEST

LOEWS CINEPLEX ODEON UPTOWN *MOVIE HOUSE*

Last of a dying breed, this classic movie house boasts one – yes, only one – big screen, perfect for viewing the special effects blockbuster of the moment. Arrive early for a coveted balcony seat.

MAP 7 A6 **A** 10 3426 CONNECTICUT AVE. NW
202-966-5400

MAP 8 | ADAMS MORGAN

VISIONS CINEMA BISTRO LOUNGE *MOVIE HOUSE*

With limited seating and no reservations, this hip cinema-cum-bistro lounge demands an early arrival. Besides the cult flicks, there's live music on Fridays.

MAP 8 E4 **A** 37 1927 FLORIDA AVE.,NW
202-667-0090 OR 202-232-5689

ARENA STAGE   TIDAL BASIN BOATHOUSE

OVERVIEW MAP

ARENA STAGE *THEATER*
Founded in 1950, the internationally renowned Arena Stage presents
new and classic American theater in its three venues: the in-the-
round Fichandler Stage, the proscenium-shaped Kreeger, and the
intimate Old Vat Room.

OVERVIEW MAP **E5** 1101 6TH ST. SW
202-488-3300

CAPITOL HILL ARTS WORKSHOP *MOVIE HOUSE*
This amateur film society shows classic movies from the 1910s
through the 1950s. A piano accompaniment jazzes up the silent
movies.

OVERVIEW MAP **E6** 545 7TH ST. SE
202-547-6839

RECREATION

MAP 1 | WESTERN MALL/FOGGY BOTTOM

ARLINGTON MEMORIAL BRIDGE

At lunchtime joggers and power walkers swarm this bridge – a symbol of North and South bound together as one great Union.

MAP 1 D2◉37 CROSSES POTOMAC AT LINCOLN MEMORIAL
703-289-2500

LADY BIRD JOHNSON PARK/LYNDON B. JOHNSON MEMORIAL GROVE

Lady Bird Johnson Park is a beautifully landscaped tribute to the woman who contributed much to outdoor beauty, with 17 acres of winding trails and pine and dogwood trees honoring our 36th president.

MAP 1 F1◉47 GEORGE WASHINGTON PKWY. AT ARLINGTON MEMORIAL
BRIDGE (VIRGINIA)
703-289-2500

LAFAYETTE SQUARE PARK

Mingle with presidential staffers on lunch in this elegant and formal D.C. park. Its location across from the White House also makes this public space a favorite of outspoken protesters.

MAP 1 A5◉15 BTWN. H ST. AND PENNSYLVANIA AVE. NW, JACKSON PL.
NW AND E. EXECUTIVE AVE.
703-289-2500

TIDAL BASIN BOATHOUSE

Paddleboats are available to rent March–October. Tone up those calf muscles, or let your partner do the work, while taking in the Jefferson Memorial.

MAP 1 E6◉46 1501 MAINE AVE. SW
202-479-2426

WEST POTOMAC PARK

This ethereal park is the setting for the Lincoln Memorial, the new World War II Memorial, the Reflecting Pool, and the famous Japanese cherry trees that bloom around the Tidal Basin each spring.

MAP 1 E3◉44 100 23RD PL. NW
703-289-2500

MAP 2 | CENTRAL MALL/SMITHSONIAN

BIKE THE SITES

Explore Washington's monuments, museums, and memorials on a guided bike tour, and see it all in 2.5 hours from the seated comfort of a cycle. They also rent bikes out so you can take your own tour.

MAP 2 C3 **40** 1100 PENNSYLVANIA AVE. NW
202-842-2453

NATIONAL GALLERY OF ART SCULPTURE GARDEN

World-class contemporary art and beautiful landscaping surround a lively public rink, open for skating November–March. A small café makes it the ideal spot to refresh when museum fatigue strikes.

MAP 2 D4 **53** BTWN. 7TH AND 9TH STS. NW, CONSTITUTION AVE. AND
MADISON DR. NW
202-737-4215

PERSHING PARK

At this downtown oasis, you can feed ducks in the pond, grab a snack, watch the world go by, or, in winter, ice skate.

MAP 2 B1 **15** 14TH ST. AND PENNSYLVANIA AVE. NW
202-737-6938

MAP 3 | CAPITOL HILL

BARTHOLDI FOUNTAIN AND PARK

Named for sculptor and Statue of Liberty designer Frederic Auguste Bartholdi, the elaborate fountain is the centerpiece of this fantastic flower-filled garden.

MAP 3 E1 **19** 1ST ST. AND INDEPENDENCE AVE. SW

D.C. DUCKS

For an off-the beaten-path experience, tour the city's streets and its waterways on this restored World War II amphibious truck. The 90-minute tours are offered mid-March–October.

MAP 3 B3 **7** UNION STATION, 50 MASSACHUSETTS AVE. NE
202-832-9800

OLD TOWN TROLLEY TOURS

Boarding at Union Station, this two-hour narrated tour of the city on a trolley-shaped bus will hit more than 100 highlights, with plenty of stops along the way.

MAP 3 B3 **8** UNION STATION, 50 MASSACHUSETTS AVE. NE
202-966-3825

BIKE THE SITES   *THE EXORCIST* STAIRS

MAP 4 | GEORGETOWN

CHESAPEAKE & OHIO CANAL NATIONAL HISTORIC PARK

At this historic park, you can take a one-hour mule-drawn boat ride up the C & O canal, April–September. Rangers dressed in period clothing tell stories and sing ballads along the way. Specialized walking tours are also available.

MAP 4 F5 ❹49 VISITORS CENTER, 1057 THOMAS JEFFERSON ST. NW
202-653-5190

CHESAPEAKE & OHIO CANAL TOWPATH

This flat hiking and biking trail meanders alongside the Potomac for 184.5 miles, becoming increasingly scenic the farther you go. If you hike 14 miles, you'll be rewarded with views of a spectacular waterfall.

MAP 4 F5 ❹48 VISITORS CENTER, 1057 THOMAS JEFFERSON ST. NW
202-653-5190

DUMBARTON OAKS PARK

Enter this 27-acre park through grand wrought-iron gates situated on a residential street. The path grows wilder as it follows along Rock Creek.

MAP 4 A4 ❹1 ENTER AT 31ST AND R STS. NW
703-289-2500

THE EXORCIST STAIRS

This 75-step (five-story) stairway – the location of the priest's fall in the famous movie – offers a dizzying run down to M Street shops and eateries. Today Georgetown athletes train by running the steps.

MAP 4 E2 ❹15 36TH AND PROSPECT STS. NW

FRANCIS SCOTT KEY BRIDGE

Take a jog on this bridge over the Potomac River for a panoramic view of the vibrant waterfront scene. The adjacent park features a bust of local legend Key with a flag similar to the banner of "Oh Say Can You See" fame.

MAP 4 F2 ❹44 34TH AND M STS. NW

WASHINGTON HARBOUR   DUPONT CIRCLE

MONTROSE PARK

During the 19th century, rope-making magnate Robert Parrott generously allowed his land to be used for local meetings and picnics. Today, the park's gardens, picnic tables, tennis courts, and 16 acres of rugged trails belong to the grateful citizenry of Georgetown.

MAP 4 B5 Ⓐ6   R ST. BTWN. 30TH AND 31ST ST. NW

WASHINGTON HARBOUR

A bustling mix of residences, boat marinas, shops, and restaurants keeps this stretch of waterfront hopping year-round. Enjoy panoramic views across the Potomac and excellent people-watching opportunities.

MAP 4 F5 Ⓐ51   31ST AND K STS. NW

MAP 5 | DUPONT CIRCLE

DUPONT CIRCLE

Stake out a patch of green to watch the people – from musicians to office workers – who congregate around the giant fountain in this lively neighborhood hub.

MAP 5 B5 Ⓐ27   MASSACHUSETTS AND CONNECTICUT AVE. NW

THOMPSON BOAT CENTER

You can join the lively summer scene on the Potomac by renting a kayak, canoe, or rowboat. Or simply watch the local racing teams practice while sipping your morning coffee.

MAP 5 E1 Ⓐ58   2900 VIRGINIA AVE. NW
202-333-9543

MAP 7 | UPPER NORTHWEST

MACOMB PLAYGROUND
The centerpiece of this residential park is a 30-foot multicolored gazebo. Tree-lined brick pathways and benches surround the multi-age play-areas.

MAP 7 B4 ✪ 16 3409 MACOMB ST. NW
309-833-4562

MAP 8 | ADAMS MORGAN

KALORAMA PARK
A favorite among local nannies, this lively neighborhood park is equipped with two playgrounds for both older and younger children.

MAP 8 D4 ✪ 21 KALORAMA RD. AND 19TH ST. NW

MARIE REED RECREATION CENTER
Head to this local recreation center for a fast-paced game of pick-up basketball. Marie Reed also features tennis courts, playground equipment, and shaded areas.

MAP 8 E5 ✪ 38 2200 CHAMPLAIN ST. NW
202-673-7768

ROCK CREEK PARK
This 1,755-acre swath of forest flanks Rock Creek and offers respite from crowds, traffic, and summer heat. Its bike and bridle paths, hiking trails, tennis courts, playgrounds, and golf course make it the perfect place to work off last night's power dinner.

MAP 8 D1 ✪ 19 3435 WILLIAMSBURG LN. NW
202-895-6000

OVERVIEW MAP

EAST POTOMAC PARK
An 18-hole public golf course – one of the country's oldest – and a giant five-piece sculpture called *The Awakening* make this park a fun and quirky destination.

OVERVIEW MAP F4 1090 OHIO DR. SW
202-426-6841

EAST POTOMAC POOL
This 50-meter outdoor pool is the perfect summer cool-off spot. Swim laps or just splash around in the reflection of Washington's monuments for a small fee ($3 for D.C. residents, $5 for nonresidents).

OVERVIEW MAP F4 1090 OHIO DR. SW
202-426-6841

COOL IT

Washington D.C. is as famous for cherry blossoms and monuments as it is notorious for squelching summer heat and humidity. But residents and repeat visitors have perfected the art of keeping cool with some secret tactics, and you can do the same. Dip your toes into the foot-friendly fountain at the **National Gallery of Art Sculpture Garden (p. 84).** Picnic under the trees in **Dupont Circle (p. 86),** or watch a pick-up soccer game from a shady bench in **Meridian Hill Park (p. 88).** If those don't do the trick, take a dive into **East Potomac Pool (p. 87)** – a couple lazy laps are guaranteed to beat the heat.

MERIDIAN HILL PARK
The lower level of this 12-acre neighborhood park (also known as Malcolm X Park), with its terraced waterfalls, broad stairways, and impressive statuary, looks like an Italian movie set. The upper level is a popular spot for Frisbee and soccer games.

OVERVIEW MAP **B4**   BTWN. 15TH AND 16TH STS. NW, EUCLID AND W STS. NW
202-462-7275

THEODORE ROOSEVELT ISLAND
Heavily forested trails surrounding a garden and 17-foot statue of Teddy Roosevelt comprise D.C.'s most sprawling monument: a 91-acre natural preserve. Pretty year-round, it's glorious in autumn.

OVERVIEW MAP **D2**   GEORGE WASHINGTON PKWY. (ACCESSIBLE ONLY
FROM VIRGINIA)

VARIOUS LOCATIONS

WASHINGTON WALKS
Whether you're fascinated by haunted houses or local secrets, these walking tours – most take place weekly April-October – are a fun and informative way to see the city. Call or visit www.washington-walks.com for schedules, descriptions, and meeting locations for the many walks.

VARIOUS LOCATIONS   202-484-1565

HOTELS

Trendsetter favorite: **HOTEL ROUGE,** p. 94

Most romantic hotel: **TABARD INN,** p. 95

Funkiest decor: **HOTEL HELIX,** p. 94

Best eavesdropping: **THE WATERGATE HOTEL,** p. 90

Best views: **HOTEL WASHINGTON,** p. 90

Best splurge: **HAY-ADAMS HOTEL,** p. 90

Best of old Washington: **MORRISON-CLARK INN,** p. 95

PRICE KEY

$ ROOMS UNDER $200

$$ ROOMS $200-300

$$$ ROOMS OVER $300

MAP 1 | **WESTERN MALL/FOGGY BOTTOM**

GEORGE WASHINGTON UNIVERSITY INN   *QUAINT* *$*

Guests can enjoy a collegiate atmosphere here, and the suite-style accommodations are an excellent value.

MAP 1 A2 ⊕ 2   824 NEW HAMPSHIRE AVE. NW
202-337-6620

HAY-ADAMS HOTEL   *GRAND* *$$$*

One of Washington's finest luxury hotels, this monument to indulgence is a favorite of visiting dignitaries. Rumors that the original owner haunts the premises add a hint of mystery to the stately surroundings – especially in winter.

MAP 1 A5 ⊕ 12   800 16TH ST. NW
202-638-6600 OR 800-424-5054

SOFITEL LAFAYETTE SQUARE   *GRAND* *$$$*

Offering a downtown location and an on-site translator, Sofitel caters primarily to business travelers who want to be in the center of it all. There's nothing frilly here, but the posh ground floor Café 15 is a swank spot to sip and sup.

MAP 1 A6 ⊕ 16   806 15TH ST. NW
202-730-8800

THE WATERGATE HOTEL   *QUAINT* *$$$*

Once scandal central, the Watergate has evolved into a stopover for the jet set: The rooms are oversized, and there's a swank health facility on site.

MAP 1 A1 ⊕ 1   2650 VIRGINIA AVE. NW
202-965-2300 OR 800-289-1555

MAP 2 | **CENTRAL MALL/SMITHSONIAN**

HOTEL MONACO   *CHIC* *$$*

With its grand European lobby, plush decor, and ultra-customized guestrooms, this whimsical downtown newcomer charms with its specialized service. Lanky patrons can request "tall rooms," and even your pooch can get pampered with gourmet doggy snacks.

MAP 2 B4 ⊕ 30   700 F ST. NW
202-628-7177 OR 877-202-5411

HOTEL WASHINGTON   *ROMANTIC* *$$*

Not only does the city's oldest hotel offer excellent, European-style accommodations for its politico-heavy clientele, it offers the best views in the city. Even if you're not a guest, order a cocktail and sightsee from the romantic rooftop Sky Terrace.

MAP 2 B1 ⊕ 12   515 15TH ST. NW
202-688-5900 OR 800-424-9540

HOTEL MONACO   BULL MOOSE B&B ON CAPITOL HILL

WILLARD INTER-CONTINENTAL   *GRAND $$$*
Dark, gilded, and steeped in tradition, this most Washington of
hotels maintains a loyal clientele with its gracious service. It is also
a historical landmark: "The Battle Hymn of the Republic" and the "I
Have a Dream" speech were written within these ornate walls.

MAP 2 B1 ⓗ14   1401 PENNSYLVANIA AVE. NW
202-628-9100

MAP 3 | CAPITOL HILL

BULL MOOSE B&B ON CAPITOL HILL   *QUAINT $*
This 10-room Victorian inn takes its name from Teddy Roosevelt's
Bull Moose Reform Party. Each room's decor reflects an episode in
TR's life, but only four have private baths.

MAP 3 D5 ⓗ16   101 5TH ST. NE
202-547-1050

DOOLITTLE GUEST HOUSE   *GRAND $*
This ornate Victorian mansion with nine fireplaces, a formal dining
room, and private baths, has a view of the Capitol from its lavish
sitting room.

MAP 3 D5 ⓗ17   506 E. CAPITOL ST.
202-546-6622

HOTEL GEORGE   *CHIC $$*
Sleek, bold, and wildly popular, this hotel is done up with modern
lines and pop art but actually occupies a 1928 edifice. The cigar-and-
billiard room and Bistro Bis restaurant add to the lively atmosphere.

MAP 3 B2 ⓗ2   15 E ST. NW
202-347-4200

HYATT REGENCY WASHINGTON ON CAPITOL HILL   *CHIC $$*
This behemoth Hyatt offers the chain's standard amenities, as well
as wireless Internet access in renovated rooms, and stands out for
its knockout atrium lobby.

MAP 3 C2 ⓗ10   400 NEW JERSEY AVE. NW
202-737-1234

MAP 4 GEORGETOWN

THE FOUR SEASONS HOTEL *CHIC $$$*
The Four Seasons imbues historic Georgetown with a breath of modernity; amenities include a three-level fitness club, in-room massage options, and some of the most exotic spa treatments in town – like the Bali Coconilla body polish.

MAP 4 E6 ⑪ 43   2800 PENNSYLVANIA AVE. NW
202-342-0444

THE GEORGETOWN INN *ROMANTIC $$*
Ideally located in the heart of Georgetown, this inn has a clubby atmosphere, mixing a touch of the Colonial era with European gentility.

MAP 4 E4 ⑪ 19   1310 WISCONSIN AVE. NW
202-333-8900

THE LATHAM HOTEL *ROMANTIC $$*
A favorite with visiting celebrities and overseas visitors, the Latham exudes European style. The hotel's acclaimed Michel Richard Citronelle restaurant gives preferential treatment to guests.

MAP 4 E5 ⑪ 37   3000 M ST. NW
202-726-5000

MAP 5 DUPONT CIRCLE

THE DUPONT AT THE CIRCLE *ROMANTIC $$*
Built in 1885, this B&B is perfectly situated on a residential street. Eight ornate rooms offer a quiet break in the big city.

MAP 5 A5 ⑪ 11   1604 19TH ST. NW
202-332-5251

HILTON WASHINGTON EMBASSY ROW *CHIC $$*
Across from the Indonesian Embassy, the Hilton is festive with colorful fabrics, art, murals, and a daily international buffet.

MAP 5 B4 ⑪ 18   2015 MASSACHUSETTS AVE. NW
202-265-1600

HOTEL MADERA *CHIC $*
This pet-friendly boutique is all about unique amenities: Make-your-own martini kits come standard in every room, specialty Screening Rooms boast fully stocked DVD libraries, and Nosh Rooms offer grocery service.

MAP 5 C4 ⑪ 30   1310 NEW HAMPSHIRE AVE. NW
202-296-7600 OR 800-430-1212

THE MANSION ON O STREET *ROMANTIC $$$*
One of the Capitol's original architects designed this exquisite 1892

THE FOUR SEASONS HOTEL   HOTEL MADERA

mansion. Art- and antique-filled, the Mansion serves as a hushed retreat for discriminating travelers.

MAP 5 B4 Ⓗ 23 2020 O ST. NW
202-496-2000

ONE WASHINGTON CIRCLE *QUAINT* *$$*
This stately property is a regular in power players' Palm Pilots. The spacious, comforting digs include suite-sized rooms, and every room offers a private balcony overlooking the neighborhood.

MAP 5 D3 Ⓗ 45 1 WASHINGTON CIR. NW
202-872-1680 OR 800-424-9671

RENAISSANCE MAYFLOWER HOTEL *GRAND* *$$*
Built for Calvin Coolidge's 1925 inauguration and situated close to the White House, this address has a lovely block-long lobby. A 2004 renovation added high-speed Internet capacity to this Marriott-company hotel.

MAP 5 D6 Ⓗ 54 1127 CONNECTICUT AVE. NW
202-347-3000

THE RITZ-CARLTON *ROMANTIC* *$$$*
This fashionably located property offers such trademark luxuries as featherbeds with Egyptian cotton sheets and thick down pillows. Outside the rooms, guests can contemplate in the courtyard's Japanese garden or reenergize in the premiere fitness facility.

MAP 5 D3 Ⓗ 44 1150 22ND ST. NW
202-835-0500

THE RIVER INN *QUAINT* *$*
Not on the river, but pretty close, these boutique-style, apartment-size suites have full kitchens. Among the communal amenities are a spa and a lounge.

MAP 5 E2 Ⓗ 59 924 25TH ST. NW
202-337-7600

THE WESTIN EMBASSY ROW *GRAND* *$$$*
Historic site of the Jockey Club and Fairfax Bar, the Westin has been pampering politicians and dignitaries since 1928. Today, patrons can enjoy the chain's signature Heavenly touches for bed and bath.

MAP 5 B4 Ⓗ 15 2100 MASSACHUSETTS AVE. NW
202-293-2100

SCANDAL SCENES

Of course, Washington is notorious for **Watergate (p. 90),** though nowadays the posh hotel seems too dignified for pettiness like eavesdropping and phone-bugging. But hotel scandals are a Washington tradition. If you're a conspiracy theorist with money to burn, check into the **Hay-Adams Hotel (p. 90),** allegedly the site of Iran-Contra meetings. Back in more innocent times, Clover Adams, the wife of the hotel's original owner, shocked her high-society friends by overdosing on cyanide in 1885. (Rumor has it that she still haunts the hallways.) Just down the street at the **Jefferson Loews Hotel (p. 95),** Clinton aide Dick Morris was photographed trysting — and sharing state secrets — with a prostitute in 1996.

MAP 6 | LOGAN CIRCLE/U STREET

THE GOVERNOR'S HOUSE HOTEL *QUAINT* $
Traditional furnishings and a popular restaurant make this a gem. The hotel's corner location provides a view from every room.

MAP 6 D2 ☰ 26 1615 RHODE ISLAND AVE. NW
202-296-2100

HAMILTON CROWNE PLAZA HOTEL – WASHINGTON D.C. *CHIC* $$
As regal as it was during the 1920s, this restored hotel with a view of Franklin Park offers the standard modern conveniences in its historical building.

MAP 6 F3 ☰ 42 1001 14TH ST. NW
202-682-0111

HOTEL HELIX *CHIC* $$
This Austin Powers-meets-the Brady Bunch hotel recalls the swinging '60s with shag carpeting, psychedelic lighting, and funky furniture perfect for its hipster clientele. Room service can bring up yummy comfort food, like grilled cheese sandwiches.

MAP 6 D3 ☰ 28 1430 RHODE ISLAND AVE. NW
202-462-9001

HOTEL ROUGE *CHIC* $
At once glam and gimmicky, this boutique attracts a young and adventurous crowd. Specialty rooms come outfitted with audiovisual accessories, computer gadgetry, or a stainless steel kitchenette, depending on whether the theme is "Chill," "Chat," or "Chow."

MAP 6 D2 ☰ 27 1315 16TH ST. NW
202-232-8000 OR 800-368-5689

JEFFERSON LOEWS HOTEL   RENAISSANCE WASHINGTON D.C. HOTEL

THE JEFFERSON LOEWS HOTEL *ROMANTIC* *$$$*
This hotel of choice for Democratic strategists is filled with original art and antiques. The restaurant and lounge – all leather and wood-paneling – is fit for a president.

MAP 6 E2 ⊕ 30   1200 16TH ST. NW
202-347-2200

THE MADISON HOTEL *CHIC* *$$*
This stunning hotel with white-glove service is a revered D.C. favorite. Adding to the dynamic vibe, local and foreign power brokers and policy makers chew the fat in its bar, restaurants, and lobby.

MAP 6 E3 ⊕ 32   1177 15TH ST. NW
202-862-1600

MORRISON-CLARK INN *GRAND* *$*
These two 19th-century townhouses mix French country and Victorian pieces under a Chinese mansard roof, and you can enjoy Southern libations on the veranda during warm-weather months. The historical ambience makes up for its proximity to a less-than-desirable neighborhood.

MAP 6 E5 ⊕ 34   1015 L ST. NW
202-898-1200

RENAISSANCE WASHINGTON D.C. HOTEL *CHIC* *$$*
This contemporary powerhouse bustles with deal makers and the high-tech crowd. The lobby can't be beat for reading *The Washington Post* over coffee.

MAP 6 F5 ⊕ 45   999 9TH ST. NW
202-898-9000 OR 800-228-9898

THE ST. REGIS *GRAND* *$$$*
Just north of the White House, the palatial 1926 St. Regis offers opulence fit for royalty (and a clientele who expects to be treated as such). Terry robes and flat-screen TVs come standard.

MAP 6 F2 ⊕ 40   923 16TH ST. NW
202-638-2626

TABARD INN *ROMANTIC* *$*
Frequented by journalists, artists, and congressional types, the 1914

ADAM'S INN   SWANN HOUSE

Tabard offers 40 rooms with period furnishings and claw-foot tubs, but no televisions, radios, or even an elevator.

MAP 6 D1 H 24   1739 N ST. NW
                  202-785-1277

THE TOPAZ HOTEL *QUAINT* $
This decidedly 21st-century boutique offers specialty yoga rooms outfitted with mats and blocks, and energy rooms equipped with exercise machines. Guests enjoying more traditional rooms receive daily horoscopes.

MAP 6 D1 H 25   1733 N ST. NW
                  202-393-3000

WYNDHAM WASHINGTON D.C. *CHIC* $$
The 12-story atrium lobby is the Wyndham's centerpiece: The hotel's stylish guest rooms, eateries, and ballrooms are all arranged around it.

MAP 6 E3 H 33   1400 M ST. NW
                  202-429-1700

MAP 8 | ADAMS MORGAN

ADAM'S INN *QUAINT* $
Fun, friendly, and inexpensive, this bed-and-breakfast beckons visitors with its cheery parlor, comfortable furnishings, and white-fenced front porch.

MAP 8 C5 H 8   1744 LANIER PL. NW
                 202-745-3600

CHURCHILL HOTEL *GRAND* $$
This elegant 1906 building makes for a refined stay. Approving locals keep the bar hopping.

MAP 8 E4 H 36   1914 CONNECTICUT AVE. NW
                  202-797-2000

HILTON WASHINGTON & TOWERS *GRAND* $$
The bustling scene of countless society galas – notably the glamorous

Washington Correspondents Dinner — this efficient corporate favorite has plenty of ballrooms and a lively bar scene.

MAP **8** E4 **H** 35   1919 CONNECTICUT AVE. NW
202-483-3000 OR 800-445-8667

JURYS NORMANDY INN   *QUAINT* $

A charming little find along Embassy Row, 75-room Jurys Normandy feels more like a friend's home than an inn. In the lobby, get cozy by the fireplace or surf the Internet for free.

MAP **8** E4 **H** 34   2118 WYOMING AVE. NW
202-483-1350

KALORAMA GUEST HOUSE   *QUAINT* $

This group of renovated Victorian townhouses offers a homey B&B escape, complete with a sunny garden and a fireplace-lit parlor.

MAP **8** D4 **H** 20   1854 MINTWOOD PL. NW
202-667-6369

OMNI SHOREHAM HOTEL   *GRAND* $$$

Adjacent to Rock Creek Park, the quiet, art deco Omni is not for party animals, despite its proximity to the zoo. Seasoned travelers will appreciate the gilded lobby, four-poster beds, and sprawling gardens.

MAP **8** C2 **H** 4   2500 CALVERT ST. NW
202-234-0700

SWANN HOUSE   *ROMANTIC* $$

Located on a residential street, this gorgeous Victorian gives you B&B individuality (inlaid floors, theme rooms), without the overly familiar aspects (all rooms have private baths). Don't miss the courtyard swimming pool in the hot summer.

MAP **8** F6 **H** 51   1808 NEW HAMPSHIRE AVE. NW
202-265-4414

THE WINDSOR INN   *ROMANTIC* $

Formerly an apartment building, this B&B boasts original art deco details in its lobby and 45 rooms that range from spartan economy to well-appointed suites.

MAP **8** E6 **H** 42   1842 16TH ST. NW
202-667-0300

OVERVIEW MAP

MANDARIN ORIENTAL   *GRAND* $$$

This posh business traveler favorite was added to Washington's waterfront in 2004. Offering panoramic views, a gourmet restaurant, and on-site spa and fitness facilities, it's an elegant landmark in an overlooked neighborhood.

OVERVIEW MAP **E4**   1330 MARYLAND AVE. SW
202-554-8588

CITY ESSENTIALS

AIRPORTS

Three major airports serve the Washington metropolitan area: Dulles International (IAD), Reagan National (DCA), and Baltimore-Washington International (BWI). The D.C. Metro system only directly services Reagan National Airport.

The Washington Flyer Coach Service Bus (www.washfly.com) provides ground transportation between Dulles and the West Falls Church Metrorail station. Tickets are sold on the bus and cost $8 one-way or $14 round-trip.

Amtrak (800-872-7245, www.amtrak.com) and the Maryland Area Rail Commuter train (MARC, 800-325-7245, www.mtamaryland.com) travel between Baltimore-Washington International and D.C.'s Union Station Monday–Friday. On the lower level, you can catch the free shuttle from airport to the train station. BWI also offers Express Metrobus service between the airport and the Greenbelt Metro station. The BWI Express/B30 bus runs every 40 minutes. Bus fare is $3, which is paid on the bus. For more information call 202-637-7000 or visit www.wmata.com.

If you take a taxi to the airport, expect to pay about $50 for a ride to Dulles, $13 to Reagan National, and $55 to BWI. Additionally, several shuttle services offer transport between the airports and hotel locations in Washington D.C. If taking a shuttle or limousine to the airport, remember to call 24 hours ahead to arrange for a pick-up.

AIRPORT EXPRESS 202-244-4606
DULLES COACH 703-444-4011
SUPERSHUTTLE 800-258-3826

ARRIVING BY TRAIN

Washington D.C.'s Union Station serves passengers arriving on Amtrak (800-872-7245, www.amtrak.com) as well as Virginia Rail Express (800-743-3873, www.vre.org) and Maryland's MARC trains (800-325-7245, www.mtamaryland.com). Union Station also connects to the Red Line of the Metro (202-637-7000, www.wmata.com) for destinations within the D.C. area.

UNION STATION
MAP 3 B3○4 50 MASSACHUSETTS AVE. NE
202-289-1908

PUBLIC TRANSPORTATION

Known locally as the Metro, Washington's Metrorail (202-637-7000, www.wmata.com) is a fun ride, clean, and quiet, with a space age feel. There is an information kiosk at every station entrance, and station managers are happy to give directions. However, be prepared for some mighty steep escalators at certain stations; one of the world's longest escalators (230 feet) is at the Wheaton station on the Red Line.

The Metro runs until midnight Sunday–Thursday and until 3 A.M. on Fridays and Saturday nights. At many stations however, the last train departs before closing time. The Metro does not have a stop in Georgetown; however, for an additional $.35 you can transfer to a Metrobus (be sure to pick up a bus transfer as you enter the Metro).

Fares range $1.35–3.90 depending on the length of the ride. One-day, unlimited ride passes cost $6.50. (Note: These day passes are only good after 9:30 A.M. on weekdays, but all day on Saturday, Sunday, and federal holidays.) A seven-day, truly unlimited pass costs $32.50. Both these passes are good for Metrorail rides only; they do not cover Metrobus fares.

For a map of the Metrorail system, pick up a free Pocket Guide at any station kiosk. Bus route maps are available in CVS pharmacies throughout the city and at the Metro Center sales office at 12th and F Streets NW.

TAXIS

Washington taxis charge by zones – there are eight in the city – rather than miles. The base fare for one zone is $5.50; crossing into another zone increases the fare. (There is a $1.50 surcharge per passenger and a $1 surcharge for rush hour fares.) Read the posted rate card inside the cab to avoid being cheated, something not uncommon in Washington. Hailing a cab is easy in downtown, but the farther you get from a busy area, the less likely it is that you will find one. Cabs are plentiful around hotels, Union Station, and the airports. You can also phone ahead and have one meet you, but this service adds $2 to your fare.

CAPITOL CAB 202-545-8900
DIAMOND CAB 202-332-6200
YELLOW CAB 202-544-1212

DRIVING AND RENTING A CAR

Driving in D.C. is a thankless task, and the notorious bumper-to-bumper traffic can reduce even the most hardened native to tears. In addition, some heavily traveled thoroughfares, such as Rock Creek Parkway, become one-way during rush hour, which can be frustrating for people unfamiliar with the area.

In addition, parking is extremely difficult in Washington, especially in popular tourist areas such as the Mall, Georgetown, and Dupont Circle. Too few spaces and too much traffic make finding a place to park frustrating and time consuming. Privately owned parking lots abound. While costly, they may save you money in the long run; parking enforcement is serious business in the capital city, with heavy fines levied for violations. Metro-operated lots require quarters during the week, but are free on weekends and federal holidays. Your best bet is to use public transportation.

If you do decide to drive, all of the major car rental chains are represented in Washington. Find them clustered together at the airports, with branches throughout the city. If you are traveling at a busy time of year, be sure to make your reservation well in advance.

ENTERPRISE RENT-A-CAR 800-736-8222 (Dulles), 202-338-0015 (downtown)
HERTZ RENT A CAR 800-654-3131 (Dulles and Reagan), 202-628-6174 (downtown)
THRIFTY CAR RENTAL 800-367-2277 (Dulles), 202-783-0400 (downtown)

VISITOR INFORMATION

The Washington D.C. Convention and Tourism Corporation (202-789-7000, www.washington.org) is the principal tourist organization in the city. Maps, brochures, and other information are available at the visitors center.

WASHINGTON D.C. VISITOR INFORMATION CENTER
MAP 2 B2   RONALD REAGAN BUILDING, 1300 PENNSYLVANIA AVE. NW
202-328-4748

WEATHER

Think warm and humid; even winter brings more than a few days of balmy weather. Summer is long, extending mid-May–late October. July and August are characterized by hot, muggy days with temperatures in the 90s, punctuated by afternoon thunderstorms. Serious cold shows up in January and February, although rarely do temperatures dip below freezing. The city is unprepared for such inclement weather; even a light dusting of snow snarls traffic. A major snowstorm every few years delights area children but closes down everything. For the current temperature and local forecast, call 202-936-1212.

HOURS

Despite its cosmopolitan veneer, Washington is a sleepy Southern town during the week, with most restaurants, coffeehouses, and clubs closing long before midnight. On weekends, the more daring among them remain open until 2:30 A.M. The

Metro runs until midnight Sunday–Thursday, and until 3 A.M. on Friday and Saturday. Additionally, the city slows down in August and during holiday weekends when Congress is out of session.

FESTIVALS AND EVENTS

JANUARY/FEBRUARY

Martin Luther King Day: Speakers recite the legendary "I Have a Dream" speech at the Lincoln Memorial. Third Monday in January. (Lincoln Memorial, 202-619-7222)

MARCH

Cherry Blossom Festival: Tourists and residents alike celebrate the 1912 gift of 3,000 cherry trees from Tokyo to the citizenry of D.C. Two unpredictable weeks in late March or early April. (Tidal Basin, 202-661-7584, www.nationalcherryblossomfestival. org)

Smithsonian Kite Festival: This airborne celebration showcases kite flying masters and a traditional Japanese *rokkaku* kite battle. First day of the Cherry Blossom Festival. (National Mall, 202-357-3030, http://kitefestival.org)

APRIL

White House Easter Egg Roll: Children roll eggs across the White House Lawn and meet the President. Call ahead for ticket information. (White House Lawn, 1600 Pennsylvania Ave. NW, 202-456-7041, www.whitehouse.gov/easter)

Filmfest DC: Once a year, D.C. channels the spirit of Cannes. This film festival showcases hundreds of new documentaries, feature films, and shorts from around the world. Late April and early May. (Multiple screening locations, 202-628-FILM, www. filmfestdc.org)

MAY

Taste of DC: Stop by this street festival and sample the diversity of D.C.'s cuisine. Admission is free. Memorial Day Weekend. (Pennsylvania Avenue btwn. 7th and 14th Sts. NW, 202-789-7002, www.tasteofdc.org)

JUNE

Smithsonian Folklife Festival: This annual celebration brings the storytellers, cuisine, artists, and musicians of different countries, cultures, and regions to the National Mall. Past years' festivals have showcased everything from music in Latino culture to maritime communities of the mid-Atlantic. Late June and early July. (National Mall, 202-275-1150, www.folklife.si.edu)

Capital Pride: D.C.'s nine-day pride festival includes a jubilant parade and raucous street festival. Mid-June. (Various locations, 202-797-3514, www.capitalpride.org)

JULY

Independence Day Celebration: D.C. lights up for the Fourth of

July. A free-to-the-public concert special features the National Symphony Orchestra and is followed by a spectacular fireworks display over the Washington Monument. July 4. (U.S. Capitol/ National Mall)

SEPTEMBER

DC Blues Festival: The D.C. Blues Society annually hosts this kickin' blues extravaganza at the Carter Barron Amphitheatre. Admission is free. Early September. (Carter Barron Amphitheater in Rock Creek Park, 202-962-0112, www.dcblues.org)

OCTOBER

Marine Corps Marathon: Whether you're a participant or a sidewalk supporter, this "People's Marathon" has prompted a weekend-long celebration since 1976. Late October. (Starts and ends near the intersection of Rt. 110 and Marshall Drive in Arlington, VA, 800-786-8762, www.marinemarathon.com)

NOVEMBER

Veterans Day at Arlington National Cemetery: Attend the annual wreath-laying ceremony at the Tomb of the Unknown Soldier – a moving tribute to our nation's veterans. November 11. (Arlington National Cemetery, 703-607-8000, www .arlingtoncemetery.org)

DECEMBER

National Christmas Tree Lighting: Thousands of spectators have flocked to the White House lawn to witness the lighting of the National Christmas Tree. Early December. (White House South Lawn, 202-208-1631, www.nps.gov/whho/pageant)

DISABLED ACCESS

All Smithsonian museums have at least one wheelchair-accessible entrance, most of them on the Mall side. Wheelchairs are available for use in most museums on a first-come, first-served basis. Restaurants, bars, theaters, and all federal buildings are equipped with restrooms accessible for travelers with disabilities. Street corners throughout the city have graded curbs for wheelchair ease.

Metro buses and subways accommodate travelers with disabilities with elevators, Braille signage, flashing signal lights, and enhanced announcements. More than 70 percent of the bus fleet is equipped with lifts, which means an automated platform lowers to the curb to facilitate boarding for passengers in wheelchairs. To be sure one of these buses comes to your stop, call 202-962-1825 before 3 P.M. on the preceding afternoon.

SAFETY

Follow the rules for any bustling major city: Always lock your car, hold tight to your belongings, and keep your wits about you. Avoid dark alleys, and don't dawdle in deserted downtown areas

at night. Be more attentive to your surroundings in Adams Morgan and Capitol Hill; common crimes are street robbery and car theft.

HEALTH AND EMERGENCY SERVICES

As in most cities in the United States, dialing 911 will connect you with police and fire emergency teams immediately. The following hospitals have 24-hour emergency rooms:

GEORGE WASHINGTON UNIVERSITY HOSPITAL
MAP 1 A3   901 23RD ST. NW
202-715-4000

GEORGETOWN UNIVERSITY HOSPITAL
MAP 4 B1   3800 RESERVOIR RD. NW
202-784-2000

PHARMACIES

CVS is the principal chain of pharmacies in D.C., with many branches throughout the city.

CVS PHARMACIES
MAP 1 A4   1901 PENNSYLVANIA AVE. NW
202-833-5702

MAP 6 E4   1199 VERMONT AVE. NW
202-737-3962

MAP 8 C6   1700 COLUMBIA RD. NW
202-234-8601

MEDIA AND COMMUNICATIONS

In this era of cell phones, pay phones can still be found on many street corners, but more than a few are apt to be out of service, broken, or otherwise unusable. More reliable are those inside museums, Metro stations, and hotel lobbies. A local call is $.50; an emergency call to 911 is free.

Etiquette requires you to turn off all electronic devices in theaters and most restaurants and music clubs. To the dismay of local residents, there is still no cell phone service in Rock Creek Park.

For post office locations and hours of operation, call 800-275-8777. A centrally located post office, not far from the White House, is the Ben Franklin station.

BEN FRANKLIN STATION
MAP 2 C2   12TH ST. AND PENNSYLVANIA AVE. NW

Two daily papers, natural rivals at opposite ends of the political spectrum, keep the locals informed: *The Washington Post* and *The Washington Times*. Both the *City Paper,* which details entertainment and nightlife, and *The Washington Blade,* which serves the gay and lesbian community, are free weeklies available at area bookstores and coffee houses.

If you don't have access to the Internet at your hotel, you can access the Internet at all locations of Kinko's, a full-service print/copy shop serving the student and business community.

Internet cafés are few and far between, as they are not part of the city's culture.

KINKO'S

MAP 4 E3 3329 M ST. NW
202-965-1414

MAP 6 F2 1612 K ST. NW
202-466-3777

CYBERSTOPCAFE

MAP 6 C2 1513 17TH ST. NW
202-234-2470

SMOKING

Smoking is permitted in bars and restaurants, although most restaurants have a nonsmoking section. Some have even voluntarily gone smoke-free. Smoking is prohibited in the Smithsonian museums and goverment buildings.

TIPPING

A general rule is to tip 15–20 percent of the final bill in restaurants and taxis. At the airport, or in a hotel, the porter or baggage handler usually receives $2 per bag.

DRY CLEANERS

LUSTRE CLEANERS OF CAPITOL HILL

MAP 3 E4 311 PENNSYLVANIA AVE. SE
202-547-1311

LOGAN CLEANERS

MAP 6 D3 1408 14TH ST. NW
202-462-2502

GEORGETOWN CLEANERS

MAP 4 E5 1070 31ST ST. NW
202-965-9655

CATHEDRAL CUSTOM CLEANERS

MAP 8 A2 3000 CONNECTICUT AVE. NW
202-234-1288

STREET INDEX

INDEX

RESTAURANTS INDEX

NIGHTLIFE INDEX

SHOPS INDEX

HOTELS INDEX

PHOTO CREDITS

Phil Shipman 2004: p. vii Skyline; Map 1 Western Mall; Map 2 Central Mall; Map 2 National Air and Space Museum Map 3 Capitol Hill; Map 3 Supreme Court; Map 4 Georgetown; Map 6 Logan Circle; Map 7 Upper Northwest; Map 7 Cineplex Odeon Uptown, Map 8 Adams Morgan; P. 3 National WW2 Memorial; p. 12 Supreme Court; p. 18 Arlington National Cemetery; p. 23 Nectar; p. 24 Bistro D'Oc; p. 27 Zaytinya; p. 29 Montmartre; p. 34 Obelisk; p. 34 Raku; p. 36 Kuna; p. 38 Spices; p. 38 Lebanese Tavern; p. 40 Meskerem ; p. 40 Teism; p. 46 Black Cat; p. 53 Apartment Zero; p. 55 Appalachian Spring; p. 60 Andre Chereky; p. 62 Nana; p. 69 Corcoran Museum of Art; p. 82 Tidal Basin Boat House.

Washington, DC Convention and Tourism Corporation: P. ix Washington Monument Courtesy of J. McGuire/ Washington CTCorp ; Map 1 Lincoln Memorial; Map 2 Smithsonian Museum; Map 4 Dumbarton Oaks; Map 4 Washington Harbor; Map 5 Dupont Circle; Map 5 Kramerbooks & Afterwords; p. 3 Jefferson Memorial; p. 7 White House Courtesy of J. McGuire/ Washington CTCorp; p. 7 FDR Memorial; p. 9 National Archives; p. 55

Eastern Market; p. 70 International Spy Museum; p. 77 JFK Center for Performing Arts; p. 77 Kennedy Center Opera House.

Other photos: Map 6 Jefferson Hotel © Lowes Hotels; P. 9 The Annunciation, Jan van Eyck, c1434/1436, Collection of the National Gallery of Art, Washington; P. 11 United States Holocaust Memorial Museum/ /Max Reid; P. 12 Bureau of Engraving and Printing Courtesy of The Department of the Treasury/Bureau of Engraving and Printing; P. 69 Arthur M Slacker Gallery © Michael Bryant/courtesy of the Arthir M. Slacker Gallery; P. 70 Hirshorn Museum and Sculpture Garden © by Lee Statsworth; P. 72 Old Stone House © National Park Srevice, Rock Creek Park; P. 80 Source Theater Company © Source Theater; P. 82 Arena Stage © Joan Marcus/ Arean Stage 1999/2000 Season- Guys and Dolls; P. 85 © Andrew Snow Bike the Sites; P. 91 © David Phelps Photography Hotel Monaco; P. 91 © Jim Tetro Photography 2000 Bull Moose B and B on Capitol Hill; P. 93 © Tom McCavera/ Four Seasons Hotel, Washington DC The Four Seasons Hotel; P. 93 © David Phelps Photography Hotel Madera; P. 95 © Burnett Studios, Inc. Renaissance Washington D.C. Hotel; P. 96 Courtesy of the Adam's Inn Adam's Inn; P. 96 © Mark Charette Swan House.

All other photos by **Erika Howsare**.

CONTRIBUTORS TO THE SECOND EDITION

KARA BASKIN *Introduction, A Day in D.C., Neighborhoods, Restaurants, Shops, Hotels*
Kara Baskin is an assistant editor at *The New Republic* magazine in Washington D.C., where she writes about pop culture. She is also a literary editor at the Gail Ross Literary Agency and a managing editor of the Jewish Rock and Roll Hall of Fame. She has written about food, travel, and culture in the Washington area for a variety of national and mid-Atlantic publications.

SCOTT DECKMAN *Sights*
Scott Deckman lives in the Capitol Hill area of Washington D.C. and works as a writer and editor in many capacities. He has contributed to *Lollipop, Virginia Living*, and the online edition of *Filter Magazine*, among others.

SYBIL DUNLOP *Performing Arts, Recreation, City Essentials*
Sybil Dunlop is a writer and a political researcher living in Washington D.C. She reviews the arts and writes about style for *Hill Rag* and *DC North*.

JONATHAN MILLER *Nightlife, Museums and Galleries*
Jonathan Miller is a freelance writer in Washington D.C.

CONTRIBUTORS TO THE FIRST EDITION
Karen Fox, Alexandra Greeley, Matt McMillen, Andrea Rouda

MOON METRO WASHINGTON D.C.

SECOND EDITION

Avalon Travel Publishing,
An Imprint of Avalon Publishing Group, Inc.

AVALON

Text and maps
© 2005 by Avalon Travel Publishing, Inc.
All rights reserved.

Metrorail System map reproduced with permission from the
Washington Metropolitan Area Transit Authority (WMATA).

ISBN: 1-56691-749-2
ISSN: 1539-090X

Editor and Series Manager: Grace Fujimoto
Design: Jacob Goolkasian
Map Design: Mike Morgenfeld
Production Coordinator: Jacob Goolkasian
Graphics Coordinator: Deb Dutcher
Cartographer: Suzanne Service
Map Editor: Kat Smith
Proofreader: Kate McKinley
Front cover photos: Washington Monument © Jeremy
Woodhouse/Getty Images; Metro Station © D2 Productions/
Index Stock Imagery

Printed in China through Colorcraft Ltd., Hong Kong
Printing History
1st edition – 2002
2nd edition – March 2005
5 4 3 2 1

Please send all feedback about this book to:
Moon Metro Washington D.C.
Avalon Travel Publishing
1400 65th Street, Suite 250, Emeryville, CA 94608, USA
email: atpfeedback@avalonpub.com
website: www.moon.com

MOON·METRO

- AMSTERDAM
- BARCELONA
- BERLIN
- BOSTON
- CHICAGO
- LAS VEGAS
- LONDON
- LOS ANGELES
- MIAMI
- MONTRÉAL
- NEW YORK CITY
- PARIS
- ROME
- SAN FRANCISCO
- SEATTLE
- TORONTO
- VANCOUVER
- WASHINGTON D.C.

**AVAILABLE AT YOUR FAVORITE
BOOK AND TRAVEL STORES**

www.moon.com

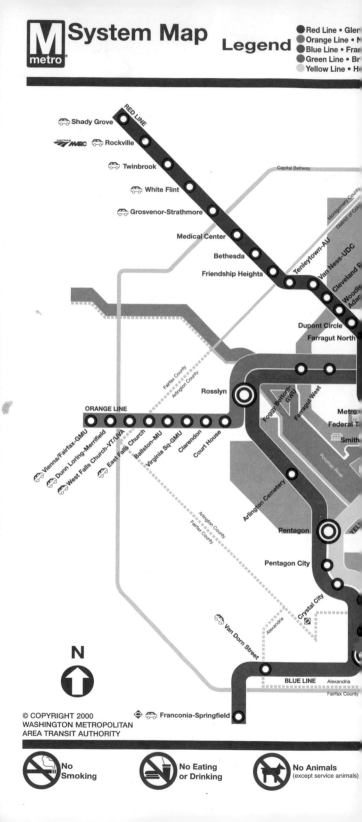